The End Is Not Yet

Yet

Standing Firm in Apocalyptic Times

John W. de Gruchy

THE END IS NOT YET

Standing Firm in Apocalyptic Times

Cover image: Coventry Cathedral in England after being bombed
in the Second World War, and the cross of reconciliation being
erected from the burnt roof timbers. Gollwitzer, Helmut / llstein
bild / Getty Images

Cover design: Laurie Ingram

Print ISBN: 978-1-5064-3157-4
eBook ISBN: 978-1-5064-3850-4

The paper used in this publication meets the minimum
requirements of American National Standard for Information
Sciences — Permanence of Paper for Printed Library Materials,
ANSI Z329.48-1984.

Manufactured in the U.S.A.

This book was produced using Pressbooks.com, and PDF
rendering was done by PrinceXML.

To my friends in the
International Bonhoeffer Society

Contents

Acknowledgments

I am grateful to several people who have played an important role in the writing and publishing of *The End Is Not Yet.* First among them are the *Dispatches* series editors, Ashley John Moyse and Scott A. Kirkland, for inviting me to participate, for their ready approval of the topic I suggested, and for their help in bringing the book to completion. I am also grateful to Will Bergkamp and Michael Gibson at Fortress Press for their friendly and professional support. It is always an honor to be a Fortress author.

My friend of long-standing, Keith Clements, readily agreed to read and comment on the final draft, and his remarks have undoubtedly added value to the outcome. Keith is one of my many friends in the International Bonhoeffer Society, which I joined in 1975, and to whom I dedicate the book. It is a remarkable Society of scholars who have become companions, both in academic research and the struggle for a more just and peaceable world. Their contribution to the understanding and continuing relevance of Bonhoeffer's legacy is immeasurable.

I am also indebted to the National Research Foundation in South Africa for its ongoing support of my academic work; to the University of Cape Town where I am an Emeritus Professor and Senior Scholar; to my colleagues in the Theological Faculty of Stellenbosch University where I am an Extraordinary Professor, and especially to Professor Robert Vosloo and the Beyers Naudé Centre.

An additional spur in writing *The End Is Not Yet* came when I was invited by Exeter University and Cathedral to give the Prideaux Lectures in May 2017. I did so under the same title and based the lectures on the book, though shortened for the occasion. So I thank Dr. Morwenna Ludlow, Head of the Theology Department at Exeter, and her colleagues for the invitation and warm welcome, and the Dean of Exeter Cathedral, Jonathan Draper, and his wife Margaret for their kind hospitality.

My biggest word of thanks goes to my newest friend, John Morris: historian, musician, and incomparable bibliophile. John's Book Cottage in Hermanus, with its heavily laden shelves and ample supply of coffee, became my regular place of call for many conversations while writing the book. And, as always, Isobel, whose busy studio is next to my study, has likewise provided encouragement and sustenance along the way. Her companionship over the years has in no small measure made it possible for me to do what I have done.

John W. de Gruchy
from Volmoed
Hermanus, South Africa
Easter 2017

Prologue: Remember the End

You will hear of wars and rumors of wars; see that you are not alarmed; for this must take place, but the end is not yet. For nation will rise against nation, and kingdom against kingdom, and there will be famines and earthquakes in various places, all this is but the beginning of the birth pangs.

—Jesus of Nazareth[1]

What happens here is something penultimate. To give the hungry bread is not yet to proclaim to them the grace of God. . . . But this penultimate thing is related to the ultimate. It is a *pen*-ultimate, before the last. The entry of grace is the ultimate.

—Dietrich Bonhoeffer[2]

1. Matt 24:6–8.
2. Dietrich Bonhoeffer, *Ethics*, Dietrich Bonhoeffer Works, vol. 6, ed. and introduction by Clifford J. Green (Minneapolis: Fortress Press, 2005), 163.

The title of this book and the headings of each chapter are questions on a recurring theme that has returned in our time with a vengeance. "The essence of the question," wrote Hans Georg Gadamer, "is the opening up, and keeping open, of possibilities."[3] Questions draw us into a process by which we examine our prejudices and assumptions, discover truth, and decide on action. So let me introduce the central questions.

Many commentators have sensed an uncanny resemblance between our time and the 1930s when the world stood on the brink of plunging into catastrophe. Is that a helpful comparison or a hindrance in understanding the present moment? After all, there are other historic parallels that might be more appropriate. Whatever the answer, Donald Trump's election as president of the United States has evoked this comparison and drawn the battle lines within which our cultural wars are being waged. It has also propelled them onto the front pages of our daily lives irrespective of where we live. Those issues central to my discussion are totalitarianism and democracy, right-wing nationalism and patriotism, globalization and economic injustice, terrorism and warmongering. But it would be misleading to blame the controversies exclusively on Trump's election. They have been part of the American and global landscape for a long time, even though now significantly heightened. Trump, like all presidents of the United States, will eventually leave

3. Hans-Georg Gadamer, *Truth and Method* (New York: Crossroad, 1988), 266.

office, but the issues will remain in one form or another. That must be kept in mind throughout what follows.

For much of the past century we have lived in a world dominated by the American Empire, the self-proclaimed protector of the capitalist "Free World" and defender of liberal democracy. When financial institutions, freedom, and democracy are threatened in the United States, it sends a shiver down the global spine. For that reason what is happening in America today is central to our conversation. But it is a global crisis we face, what some theologians call a "*kairos* moment."[4] The great Hebrew prophets of social justice spoke truth to power at such critical times. They did not try to convince their hearers of abstract theological truth but offered "images of new possibility" that were subversive of the status quo.[5] Such prophecy does not predict the end times, as fundamentalists assume, but is a call to repentance in order to prevent national and international disaster.

Given the fact that *Dispatches* is a series of theological, and specifically Christian, texts, we have to ask what God is doing at this moment in history. How is it possible to justify faith in God given the power of evil and the immense suffering of so many people across

4. John W. de Gruchy, "Kairos Moments and Prophetic Witness: Towards a Prophetic Ecclesiology," in *HTS Teologiese Studies / Theological Studies* 72, no. 4 (2016).

5. Walter Brueggemann, *Theology of the Old Testament: Testimony, Dispute, Advocacy* (Minneapolis: Fortress Press, 1997), 625–26.

the globe, from natural disasters to acts of terror? Why is God silent when we desperately need to hear the word of authentic prophets who speak to our situation with authority and insight, and so lead us and the next generation into the future? And why are Christians so divided in their response to Trump's election and the issues that now face us?

Christians have, of course, long been divided by denomination and their attitudes toward social and political issues.[6] But today, the polarities between so-called liberal and conservative Christians have become freshly divisive, even within families. These two terms are now rather threadbare from overuse, and like all typologies they never quite represent the facts on the ground. In terms of my narrative, I prefer to speak about Catholic traditionalists, some of whom are key members of Trump's inner circle, who resist many of the decisions of the Second Vatican Council and find some of the views of Pope Francis too progressive or radical. Then there are the ecumenical progressives and evangelical fundamentalists found in many if not all denominations. This categorization by no means covers the field, but for my purposes it must suffice.

"Ecumenical progressives" is a description that speaks for itself, whether it refers to Protestants, Catholics, or evangelicals, but a few more words are

---

6. See Sydney E. Ahlstrom, *A Religious History of the American People* (Garden City, NY: Doubleday, 1975); H. Richard Niebuhr, *The Social Sources of Denominationalism* (New York: Meridian, 1960).

necessary to clarify what is meant by evangelical-fundamentalism.[7] For starters, it is important to note that not all evangelicals are fundamentalists even though the two are invariably merged in the media and popular discourse. In Europe "evangelical" refers to Protestants and specifically Lutherans, and most of them would be horrified to be labeled fundamentalists. So I will avoid the word "evangelical" and simply speak about Christian fundamentalists whose basic premise is the inerrant authority of the Bible and the rejection of any attempt to critically restate its meaning for today. They are also usually archconservatives on political and social matters, using a random selection of biblical texts to support their claims. But most significantly for the purposes of this book, most fundamentalists embrace literal apocalyptic interpretations of history centered around the second coming of Jesus.

As a teenager growing up in South Africa in the 1950s I was briefly a fundamentalist, and in those circles expectations were high that Jesus would return soon to sort out the world's problems and usher in the millennium. The end was nigh and we had to prepare to meet our God. Our main mission in life was to get people saved and ready for judgment day. The fundamentalists I knew back then were devout people, but narrow in their views, kept their faith separate from politics, or, if white, supported Apartheid.

7. George M. Marsden, *Understanding Fundamentalism and Evangelicalism* (Grand Rapids: Eerdmans, 1991).

I soon shed my fundamentalist worldview and about fifty years later I wrote *Being Human: Confessions of a Christian Humanist* in which I traced my journey toward a different understanding of what it means to be a Christian.[8] I have not lost my Christian commitment, and retain my respect for the authority of the Bible in its witness to the God revealed in Jesus Christ. I have also discovered that the Bible says as much about economic justice as it does about prayer, a great deal about love for the "other" and even the enemy, and generally portrays God as the champion of the oppressed. Jesus certainly embraced all the people whom the religious teachers of his day excluded and shunned.

In February 2010, our eldest son Steve drowned in a river accident. That tragic event threatened to shatter my wife Isobel's and my own faith. In response, I wrote *Led into Mystery*.[9] I had suddenly come face to face with the end to which we are all being drawn. I also became aware that I was being led deeper into the mystery we name God. This journey distinguishes me from those secularists for whom death is the end of the human story, as well as those Christians who disparage justice and peace on earth in pursuing bliss with fellow believers in some remote afterlife.

The End Is Not Yet, the third volume in what has now become a trilogy, builds on these two earlier volumes.

8. John W. de Gruchy, *Being Human: Confessions of a Christian Humanist* (London: SCM, 2006).
9. John W. de Gruchy, *Led into Mystery: Faith Seeking Answers in Life and Death* (London: SCM, 2013).

It is an attempt to confess faith in God, despite the shocking realities of the world in which we live today, within the framework of the eschatology that sustains Christian hope. This means interpreting present reality in terms of "the end," or the mystery of God's future, already disclosed in Jesus the Christ.

I have dedicated the book to my friends in the International Bonhoeffer Society, many of them Americans. At this "*kairos* moment" I stand in solidarity with them as they seek to respond to what is happening, drawing on Bonhoeffer's legacy. I was a graduate student in Chicago in 1963–64 when I first began to study Bonhoeffer in depth and reflected on his significance for both the Civil Rights Movement that was reaching a crescendo at that time, and the emerging church struggle in South Africa back home. Having subsequently spent much time in America I have come to understand its cultural complexity, as well as both its fault-lines and its undeniable achievements. Fortunately, America's greatness does not depend on Trump's promises, or his ability to keep them.

I owe a great deal to many Americans, not least some of my finest teachers and mentors. So while I despair of much in contemporary American culture and politics, I know there are many in America who stand firm against the current plunge into fervent right-wing nationalism, unrestrained capitalism, and uncritical patriotism. May this "*kairos* moment" be a wake-up call to others also to stand firm for America's truly democratic values and not surrender its soul to the undermining forces at work. As the celebrated American author Marilynne Robinson said in an interview on the election of Trump: "I'm frankly sort of glad that this bizarre thing has happened. Trump has brought us to a state where we will have to do a lot of very basic thinking about how our society goes on from this point."[10]

It is undoubtedly too early to assess Trump's presidency. For the sake of America and the rest of the world we can only hope that the outcome will be better than some critics forecast, and what I myself fear. In an article published shortly after Trump's election, the former Archbishop of Canterbury, Rowan Williams, said that while we do not know what Trump will do, and while we may give him the benefit of the doubt, we "have seen elsewhere how extremists have been elected with the optimistic collusion or tolerance of those who believe that such people can be 'managed' in office; and we have seen them discover, bitterly and too late, their error."[11] While it is difficult not to "play the man rather than the ball" because in his case the two are so connected, my interest is in unpacking and evaluating the issues rather than the person who has thrust them into the headlines.

10. In an interview with Robert McCrum, "From Marilynne Robinson to Richard Ford, Six Writers in Search of Trump's America," *The Guardian*, January 15, 2017.
11. Rowan Williams, "Mass Democracy Has Failed—It's Time to Seek a Humane Alternative," *New Statesman*, November 17, 2016.

If America is the focus of much of my discussion, political developments in France and especially Germany, from the French Revolution to the collapse of the Weimar Republic and the rise of Hitler, provide the backstory. In the course of this often-violent history, France built a secular democracy committed to "liberty, equality, and fraternity," while Germany chose the path of authoritarian rule. That foreshadows much of what has happened since then from the First World War to the formation of the European Union, and helps explain why many fear that the looming breakup of the EU would be a disaster for the future of the Continent and for global democracy as well.

South Africa provides a good vantage point from which to sketch this complex story and participate in the conversation. But it is also a place whose colonial past has made it a part of the dark side of Western history, and whose post-apartheid dispensation has plunged it deeply into the global concerns that are central to what follows. South Africa has achieved much during the past twenty years or so, but it still struggles to overcome the legacy of its colonial and racist past, while dealing at the same time with severe economic and social challenges exacerbated by global factors, political ineptitude, and corruption. South Africa cannot separate itself from either the world in general or from Africa in particular, nor can those of us engaged in intellectual and theological reflection avoid the challenge of decolonization.

Dietrich Bonhoeffer continues to inform the way in which I do theology. Many agree that he speaks to our contemporary situation with new relevance because the crisis we face bears an uncanny and frightening resemblance to Germany in the 1930s. Bonhoeffer, I believe, is a prophet for our time.[12] This does not mean that we should equate America today with the Nazi Germany in which he bore witness, but rather that we should consider how he understood his faith and his responsibilities as a citizen in his own times and discern where his words might resonate for us today."[13] In doing so we should, with Bonhoeffer, always remain hopeful but not "be surprised if things take a decisive turn for the worst." That "sort of complacency is incompatible with faithful Christian witness. . . ."[14]

Towards the end of his life Bonhoeffer began to write his *Ethics*, the book he regarded as his most important. Tragically he was arrested, imprisoned, and killed before he could finish it, a task left to his friend Eberhard Bethge. But one key insight in his *Ethics* informs my discussion: that is the distinction Bonhoeffer made between the "penultimate" and the "ultimate," between the "things before the end" and "the

12. John W. de Gruchy, "Bonhoeffer: Prophet for Our Time, Kairos Theology in a Global Era," paper presented at the Twelfth International Bonhoeffer Congress, July 6–10, 2016, Basel, Switzerland.

13. Statement issued by the International Bonhoeffer Society, English-language section, February 2017, http://religionnews.com/2017/02/03/statement-issued-by-the-board-of-directors-of-the-international-bonhoeffer-society/.

14. Stephen R. Haynes, *The Huffington Post*, November 28, 2016.

end" itself.[15] In the penultimate, Bonhoeffer tells us, we can never act with pure motives and intentions as though we had all the answers, or do so as if it is our task to establish God's kingdom on earth here and now by whatever means available. Such an approach "sees only the ultimate," and therefore disregards the penultimate. The alternative is the way of compromise, but that is failing to act responsibly here and now with "the end" in sight.

In the immediate aftermath of the Second World War, with Berlin and much of Germany destroyed, Paul Tillich wrote words that speak to us now: "We happen to live in a time when very few of us, very few nations, very few sections of the earth, will succeed in forgetting the end. For in these days the foundations of the earth do shake."[16] In speaking of "the end" Tillich used the Greek word *telos*, hence "teleology," the attempt to understand the present from the perspective of the end, or in terms of its fulfillment. For Christians this refers not only to the purpose of life, but also to the completion of God's redemptive purposes in Christ who is both the beginning and the end of creation.[17] This is the good news of God's kingdom in which we put our trust and hope, and to which we witness in this time of political crisis and despair.

15. Bonhoeffer, *Ethics*, 146–70.
16. Paul Tillich, "The Shaking of the Foundations," a sermon preached in 1946 and included in Tillich, *The Shaking of the Foundations* (Harmondsworth, UK: Penguin, 1964), 20–21.
17. See Rev 22:13.

I have long been engaged in theological reflection on history and politics; in doing so I espouse what Robin Lovin, a Bonhoeffer scholar and political ethicist, once called the "Unapologetic Principle." He was referring to the legacy of Reinhold Niebuhr whose theological engagement with political realities shaped a generation in the United States, including a young student named Bonhoeffer, in the mid-twentieth century.[18] The "Unapologetic Principle" is simply this: every discipline has its own integrity, among them political science, history, and theology, and each contributes to public discourse best when it does so out of its own convictions, offering its own insights, and trusting that it will help make the world a better place. In that spirit, I offer these reflections as part of the conversation into which we have all been drawn by the times in which we live.

18. Robin W. Lovin, *Christian Realism and the New Realities* (Cambridge: Cambridge University Press, 2008), 129.

PART I

The Times in Which We Live

1

Is This the End?

Have there ever been people in history who in their time, like us, had so little ground under their feet, people to whom every possible alternative open to them at the time appeared equally unbearable, senseless, and contrary to life? Have there ever been those who like us looked for the source of their strength beyond all those available alternatives?

—Dietrich Bonhoeffer[1]

1. Dietrich Bonhoeffer, *Letters and Papers from Prison*, Dietrich Bonhoeffer Works, vol. 8 (Minneapolis: Fortress Press, 2010), 38.

> Things fall apart; the centre cannot hold;
> Mere anarchy is loosed upon the world . . .
> Surely some revelation is at hand;
> Surely the Second Coming is at hand . . .
>
> —W. B. Yeats[2]

Chinua Achebe, the distinguished Nigerian author, died the day I began writing this chapter. His novel, *Things Fall Apart*, written sixty years ago, calls to mind W. B. Yeats's poem "The Second Coming." Its opening lines have since become an overused mantra, yet few others capture so well the cultural despair of these days in relation to the themes of this book. The center is not holding, the left is faltering, and the right is in ascendency. We fear both the anarchy let loose and the militarist solutions looming in response. Good leaders lack conviction, "while the worst are full of passionate intensity."

Yeats wrote against the background of the struggle for Irish independence shortly after the First World War; Achebe, as the winds of decolonization swept through sub-Saharan Africa.[3] I write as a South African twenty-two years after the end of Apartheid and twenty after the Constitution of the new democratic South Africa was signed into law by Nelson Mandela. Back then the Cold War was over, democracy was

2. William Butler Yeats, "The Second Coming," *The Norton Anthology of Poetry*, ed. Mary Jo Salter, Margaret Ferguson, and Jon Stallworthy, 4th edition (New York: W. W. Norton, 1970), 1091–92.

3. Chinua Achebe, *Things Fall Apart* (London: Heinemann, 1958).

spreading across the world, and globalization was moving into top gear. Future prospects seemed bright as more affluent nations adopted New Millennium goals for uplifting those that were poor. The center was holding. Dreams of a new world were coming true. That seems a long time ago.

Apocalyptic Times

Before his death Jesus told his disciples he would return soon to usher in God's kingdom or, better, God's reign of justice and peace on earth. Ever since, many Christians have tried to determine whether current wars and natural disasters are signs of Jesus's imminent second advent. Time and again they have been disappointed, but speculation has not ceased and, in times of crisis, expectations rise to new levels. In such times, countless sermons refer to current "wars and rumors of war" and "famines and earthquakes in various places," as proof that the "end times" are approaching. This is the stuff on which fundamentalist predictive prophecy thrives, but is this the prophetic word we need to hear?

It is easy to dismiss apocalyptic views as the beliefs of a few fundamentalist cranks on the fringes of Christianity. But the texts from which they draw their inspiration are embedded in the Bible, and many literally accept their authority in interpreting historical events. The fact is, Christianity gestated in an apocalyptic

5

milieu, and apocalyptic movements have regularly sur-
faced during its history. The Book of Revelation, which
was written to encourage Christians to persevere in
hope in such times, ends with the confident acclamation of the risen Christ: "Surely, I am coming soon!"
The responsive cry, "Amen. Come Lord Jesus!"[4] still
echoes when Christians celebrate the Eucharist. Belief
in the Second Coming is part of our creed, a symbol of
hope that in the end, as Julian of Norwich envisioned
in fourteenth-century war-torn England, "all shall be
well."[5]

Although many major Christian thinkers up to the
fourth century believed that Christ would soon return
to establish his reign of a thousand years, or the millennium, referred to in the Apocalypse of St. John,[6]
Christians soon began to accept that the end was not
imminent. Therefore they had to rethink their
response to Jesus's promise of an early return. So less
apocalyptic ways of understanding the "end times"
began to develop. From the fourth century, some
began to equate the Catholic Church itself with the
coming kingdom of God, a conviction that underlies
the medieval notion of the Holy Roman Empire as
"Christendom."

Within Christendom, millenarian movements were
soon regarded as a threat to the state. Apocalyptic

4. Rev 22:20.
5. Julian of Norwich, "The Thirteenth Revelation," *Showings* (New York: Paulist, 1978), 225.
6. Rev 20:2–7.

ideas, such as the dispensationalist views proclaimed by the Franciscan friar Joachim de Fiore in twelfth-century Florence, or those reforming movements that depicted the pope as the anti-Christ referred to in the Book of Revelation, were forcefully suppressed. Despite this, they regularly erupted into the public arena in times of social and political unrest, as they did in England during the Civil War in the seventeenth century, and through much of the nineteenth century in the United States. In the process, two distinct under-standings of the "end times" emerged: premillennial and postmillennial.

Premillennialists expect Christ to return to inaugu-rate his reign on earth before the final judgment of the world. Many fundamentalists who espouse this view are also "dispensationalists," believing that God acts in ways that are particular to seven distinct historical epochs, beginning with the age of "Adam before the Fall" and ending with the millennium. According to them, we live today in the "age of grace," which extends from Pentecost to the return of Christ when he will redeem his followers from the world before the catastrophic "end time."

Postmillennialists, by contrast, believe that God is at work establishing his kingdom in the world through his Spirit active in the missionary activity of the church. If premillennialists are somewhat pessimistic, believing that the world will get worse before the end, postmillennialists are hopeful that the world will get better through revivals, missionary outreach, and social action. This is similar to the position of some fundamentalists who wish to build a theocratic rather than a just secular society; but it was also the basis for the "social gospel" in America, the idea that the kingdom of God could and should be extended by working for justice and peace.

The idea that the world might come to an end, whether soon or in the distant future, is not only the view of Christians, it is also a view expressed from one end of the ideological spectrum to the other, though understood differently. Following the collapse of Soviet Communism in 1989, and the seeming victory of liberal democracy and global capitalism, the neoconservative American Francis Fukuyama argued that the "end of history" had arrived.[7] That is not the same as saying that the end of the world has arrived, but certainly Fukuyama meant the end of history as we know it. Fukuyama could not have been more wrong. Starting at the same historic moment, the Slovenian neo-Marxist philosopher Slavoj Žižek has more recently taken a very different and more sobering position. Hope for a more just world has collapsed, he says, and "the noble struggle for freedom and justice has turned out to be little more than a craving for bananas and pornography."[8] Then there are those who, like the

---

7. Francis Fukuyama, *The End of History and the Last Man* (London: Penguin, 1992).

8. Slavoj Žižek, *Living in the End Times* (London-Dublin: Verso, 2011), vii.

economist James Rickards, in the light of the current financial crises, proclaim that "this is the end." And because governing elites will not surrender privilege without a fight, there "will be," he says, "blood in the streets, not metaphorically but literally. Neofascism will emerge, order responding to disorder, with liberty lost."[9]

But the notion that the end of the world is approaching also has the support of scientists who warn us about the ecological disasters we face. This does not carry with it the hopeful vision of a "new earth" as depicted in the Book of Revelation, but either way, the liberal belief in inevitable progress, a core conviction of modernity, now appears untenable. As Satyajit Das reminds us, the recession that followed the banking collapse in 2007 demonstrated "that perpetual growth and progress is an illusion."[10] This does not mean that development is unnecessary, but progress as we have come to understand it is not sustainable in a world where energy, food, and water are increasingly scarce commodities. Present-day demographics, escalating violence, the beating of war drums, the fight against terrorism, financial turbulence, natural disaster, and environmental decay are producing a cumulative effect that is frighteningly apocalyptic in size and scope. Whether as an "act of God" or one of human stu-

9. James Rickards, *The Road to Ruin: The Global Elites' Secret Plan for the Next Financial Crisis* (New York: Penguin, 2016), 53.

10. Satyajit Das, *A Banquet of Consequences: The Reality of Our Unusually Uncertain Economic Future* (London: Pearson, 2015), 283.

pidity, or a combination of both, the end could come at any moment.

Sermons about the end times do not need, then, to create a receptive audience; their modern audience has been brought up on movies, computer war games, and media reports that have made the fulfillment of their prophecies virtual reality. Such is the uncertain and fearful context in which we live. The "Four Horsemen of the Apocalypse"[11]—plague, war, famine, and death—have returned in our time with frightening intensity. Only now, in Žižek's words, they are the ecological crisis, the consequences of the biological revolution, imbalances within the capitalist system, and struggles over resources along with the "explosive growth of social divisions and exclusions."[12]

Before going further I need to clarify the nature of apocalyptic literature, such as the Revelation of St. John.[13] It is not a predictive text about what will literally happen in historical time, but an attempt to understand the present time as a battleground between the powers of good and evil, between God and Satan, with a firm anticipation that God will ultimately be the victor and the world will be transformed for the better. The whole point of John's Apocalypse is to assure believers that evil will not triumph, and to exhort them to persevere and remain faithful.

11. Rev 6:1–8.
12. Žižek, *Living in the End Times*, x.
13. A useful overview is Craig R. Koester, *Revelation and the End of All Things* (Grand Rapids: Eerdmans, 2002).

Apocalyptic literature, in other words, is highly symbolic, and therefore the attempt to read into the Book of Revelation historical events of the past or present indicates a misunderstanding of the genre. To speak of the apocalyptic times in which we live does not mean that certain prophecies in the Bible are literally coming true, even if many allusions are frighteningly realistic. In these times in which we live the struggle between good and evil, between justice and oppression, between truth and lies, is becoming intense, thus demanding great vigilance and faithfulness on the part of those seeking to be faithful disciples of Jesus. But the language and symbols used are metaphorical. When taken as though they refer to historical people and events, we end up with an ideology, apocalypticism, something akin to what Bonhoeffer called "ethical fanaticism."[14]

Apocalypticism is not simply the pervasive mood that takes hold of many people in troubled times, or the key for interpreting current events. Its language and symbols are also employed to increase fear and hatred of the "others" as the enemy,[15] and harness support for right-wing agendas that purport to engage and defeat the forces of the anti-Christ or whoever else is identified with the current evil empire. Apart from Christian apocalypticism, which is mirrored in

14. Bonhoeffer, *Ethics*, Dietrich Bonhoeffer Works, vol. 6, ed. Clifford J. Green (Minneapolis: Fortress Press, 2005), 78.
15. Umberto Eco, *Inventing the Enemy* (London: Harvill Secker, 2012), 1–21.

some forms of Judaism and Islam, Žižek also writes about New Age and techno-digital-posthuman apocalypticism. The latter-two are pervasive among the younger generation but more powerfully feed into the general cultural despair of our time. Nonetheless, the Christian version, which Žižek labels "the most ridiculous," is still dangerous because of its radical millenarian logic and political clout.[16]

The fact is, such views are held by some members of the U.S. Congress and many of Trump's supporters. This is sobering, for it is one thing for Christians to believe that Christ will return soon and that "born-again" Christians will govern, or that the Messiah will come to Jerusalem when the Temple is rebuilt, but quite another for politicians to base their Middle Eastern policy on apocalyptic passages in Scripture, convinced that the Battle of Armageddon will take place soon. War in the Middle East, some even believe, will speed up the return of Jesus, though it is more likely to accelerate the destruction of the planet and result in the slaughtering of the innocent. And precisely because the conflict in the Middle East and the situation in Israel/Palestine is so much at the center of political developments, as it has always been at the center of apocalyptic readings of history, so the Israeli-Palestinian question has become a focal point of concern in much the same way as "the Jewish question" was for Bonhoeffer.[17]

16. Žižek, *Living in the End Times*, 336–37.

Apocalypticism is, however, more than a source of confusion and anxiety, it is also a cultural neurosis that accompanies mass disappointment when optimistic dreams about the future fail to materialize.[18] As Joyce Cary put it in his novel *Except the Lord*: "My father was one of those who waited confidently for the second coming of Christ, a doctrine appealing strongly to many lost and bewildered souls. . . ."[19] Apocalyptic images that daily confront us should galvanize us to action, not reduce us to fearful impotence. But we should also be wary that in such times, when fears are at their height and anger with incumbent elites is on the rise, there is usually a demand for strong totalitarian or Messianic leaders who can assuage fear and get the job done that needs to be done—whatever that may be. As Jesus himself warned his disciples, false messiahs arise to convince us that the end is near in order that we should follow them.[20] But their promises are not to be trusted. Yeats expressed this graphically in the final lines of his poem when he asked:

> . . . what rough beast, its hour come round at last,
> Slouches towards Bethlehem to be born?[21]

17. John W. de Gruchy, "Bonhoeffer's Legacy and Kairos-Palestine," *Journal of Theology for Southern Africa* 149 (July 2012): 56–69; Naim S. Ateek, "A Concluding Theological Postscript," in *Zionism and the Quest for Justice in the Holy Land*, ed. Donald E. Wagner and Walter T. Davis (Eugene, OR: Wipf & Stock, 2014), 217–20.

18. Paul Tillich, *The Courage to Be* (New Haven: Yale University Press, 1952), 70.

19. Joyce Cary, *Except the Lord* (London: Michael Joseph, 1953), 5.

20. See Luke 21:8.

21. Yeats, "The Second Coming," *The Norton Anthology of Poetry*, 1091.

False messiahs do not encourage us to persevere in the struggle for justice and peace, they tell us to trust in their leadership and their promises of a utopia in which they will right all wrongs. "Trust me!" is their signature tune. Such political Messianism, which uses democratic liberties to gain mass popular support for a promised utopia is, as J. L. Talmon has shown, the origin of what he calls "totalitarian democracy,"[22] a subject about which I will say more in chapter 3.

There is always a ready response to utopian promises, even though the more level-headed know they cannot be fulfilled this side of eternity. This does not mean that utopian thinking does not fulfill an important function. In its vision of the coming of God's reign, Christianity is undoubtedly utopian. This energizes hope in action and strengthens endurance. After all, nobody wants to live in a dystopia. That is quite literally not a good place to be. But insofar as a perfect society is always beyond our reach, utopian thinking and Messianic pretensions unchecked by critical realism lead to totalitarianism even if by default or democratic means. Great and holy causes can, in Rabbi Jonathan Sacks' apt turn of phrase, turn utopian dreams "into nightmares of hell."[23] Reflecting on Nazism in July 1940, just a few months into the war, the British author J. B. Priestly wrote these somber words:

22. J. L. Talmon, *The Origins of Totalitarian Democracy* (London: Sphere Books, 1970).
23. Jonathan Sacks, *Not in God's Name: Confronting Religious Violence* (New York: Schocken, 2015), 10.

IS THIS THE END?

... reduced to its very simplest but profoundest terms, this is a war between despair and hope; for Nazism is really the most violent expression of the despair of the modern world. . . . It's the black abyss at the end of the wrong road. It's a negation of the good life. It is at heart death-worship.[24]

Ressentiment and Despair

Media images often portrayed Trump's supporters as racist chauvinists attracted by his rhetoric that appealed to their baser instincts. These certainly constituted his "shock-troops," those supporters who roughed-up reporters, critics, and people of color. But there were many others, the majority perhaps, who voted for Trump out of anger at the present status quo, a dislike of the political establishment, and fear for the future. Some might have been gullible, ill-informed, easily misled, or opportunistic, but they were not all racist idiots. What probably united them most was their desire for "law and order" in the cities and on the streets of America, peace across the globe, and respect for authority and conservative morality. Trump got their vote because they felt that all other hopes of fulfilling their dreams had slipped from their grasp and the nation's leaders in politics, business, and banking could not care less, or do what was necessary. So despite Trump's confusing, contradictory, and some-

24. J. B. Priestly commenting on the rise of Nazism, July 7, 1940, in *Postscripts* (London: Heinemann, 1940), 25.

15

times hate-filled and vulgar message, despite his lifestyle, which probably evoked as much envy as distaste among many, he gave them reason to hope and a cause with which to identify. He was the strong leader on whom they could rely. He promised utopia. Trumpism would make America great again.

The Danish philosopher Søren Kierkegaard observed the same tendencies in nineteenth-century Europe, which he described with the French word *ressentiment*. Nothing, he wrote, better expressed the "continuously grumbling exasperation" that engenders a hate that is "big with an infinite number of hostile intentions." *Ressentiment* is like a poison, which neutralizes what is good and allows "all that is low and despicable" to come to the fore.[25] This hostility arises out of frustration, is directed against a perceived enemy, and prevents critical self-reflection or the recognition of personal failure and guilt. Would-be dictators, the "beasts slouching towards Bethlehem" in Yeats's image, capitalize on *ressentiment* because they, too, are its casualties. But they also have the demonic desire and ability to manipulate paranoia for their own ends, inventing scapegoats, and cultivating hatred.

Fritz Stern, a Jewish refugee from Nazi Germany and later a professor of history at Columbia University in New York, was deeply disturbed about this same

25. Søren Kierkegaard, *The Present Age and Two Minor Ethico-Religious Treatises*, trans. Alexander Dru and Walter Lowrie (London: Oxford University Press, 1940), 23–24. See also Friedrich Nietzsche, *The Genealogy of Morals*, trans. Francis Goffling (New York: Doubleday, 1956), §§ 10–11.

sequence of events in Europe in the twentieth century. In *The Politics of Cultural Despair* (1961), he wrote about the political *ressentiment* and revolutionary discontent that arose in the early 1930s amid "declining liberalism . . . the impact of the depression and the enfeeblement of democracy." This "rebellion against modernity," Stern said, "lies latent in Western society." He went on to say that while "its confused, fantastic program, its irrational and unpolitical rhetoric" might embody genuine but misguided aspirations, it leads to tyranny.[26]

Although Stern was writing specifically about Nazism, he had an eye on the cultural pessimism and political malaise that was pervading much of American society in the sixties at the time of the Vietnam War and the Civil Rights Movement. Could there be, he asked in his concluding paragraph, another Third Reich? "Can one abjure reason, glorify force, prophesy the age of the imperial dictator, can one condemn all existing institutions, without preparing the triumph of irresponsibility?"[27] Once rationality and critical thought give way to the will-to-power, as Friedrich Nietzsche called it, totalitarianism rears its head, democratic processes and institutions are ignored or rejected, hatred of "the other" is encouraged, force becomes the popular will, and irresponsible actions follow at all levels. It may not be the tyranny of one

26. Fritz Stern, *The Politics of Cultural Despair: A Study in the Rise of Germanic Ideology* (New York: Doubleday, 1965), 13; see also Hannah Arendt, *The Origins of Totalitarianism* (New York: Harcourt Brace Jovanovich, 1973), 305–40.

27. Stern, *The Politics of Cultural Despair*, 361.

man, a Mussolini or Hitler, a Stalin or a Pol-Pot, but it could be the tyranny of an oligarchy of right-wing authoritarian nationalists in South Africa, Israel, Turkey, the United States, or any number of other countries across the globe.

When peoples and nations look into the abyss not quite knowing what to do next, they generally elect strong illiberal leaders, or allow them to grasp power. We cannot blame Trump for being elected. He was shrewd enough to grasp the significance of the prevailing mood of the disaffected, and had the capacity to seize the opportunity to fulfill his ambition. The fact that he was also the embodiment of questionable values was not an issue for his base. For most people who responded to him, such values had long been seeping into the American psyche and were already widely applauded as the hallmarks of individual and corporate success. Trump embodied, for them at least, the much-vaunted "American way of life": extravagance, showmanship, an ability to beat the system, evade the taxman, and win at all costs. In concluding his comprehensive study of Trump, Michael D'Antonio puts his finger on this critical point:

> Donald Trump is not a man apart. He is, instead, merely one of us writ large. Given his intense desire to distinguish himself as special, if not sui generis, he is likely to find this conclusion disturbing. It is, for the rest of us too.[28]

But Trumpism was also convincing for right-wing nationalists, Catholic traditionalists, Protestant fundamentalists, and white supremacists in its denunciation of those they deem the enemies of America, thereby encouraging hate for easily identifiable scapegoats on whom blame and guilt could be cast. Without an "enemy" to fight, now no longer Communists and Catholics, but Muslims, Mexicans, liberal intellectuals, and "the Media," America could not regain its "true" identity and become great again. Such demons that lurk beneath the surface of American culture were brought to the surface and put on display during the election campaign, and there is no sign after a few months into the new presidency of any willingness to have them exorcised. So the challenge facing us in rejecting Trump's presidential game plan is how we should respond to both the implementation of the policies he is pursuing that reflect the gut-feelings of his grass-roots supporters, and to the ideological designs of those he has gathered around him as advisors and members of his cabinet.

Most of this inner circle are billionaires, right-wing in their political orientation, Catholic traditionalists or devout fundamentalists, white and male. Whether or not Trump himself will be consistent or coherent, the path he is taking to make America great is transparent from this choice of advisors. American national-

28. Michael D'Antonio, *The Truth about Trump* (New York: St. Martin's, 2016), 346.

ist and economic supremacy, Americanism we might call it, is the agenda and goal. So while Trump may not be a tyrant in the sense that Hitler was, he is a demagogue guided by business interests or right-wing ideologists, but also mirroring "the worst qualities of a mob."[29] That is how he has functioned in business and on TV reality shows. And now, whatever the constitutional checks and balances there may be on the president of the United States, Trump has considerable firepower as incumbent of the White House.

In short, what is emerging has worrying features reminiscent of totalitarian nationalisms that have dotted the political landscape in Europe since the Napoleonic era, posing not just a threat to democratic governance but also to world peace. When considered in relation to the rise of extremist terror, and to the shaky balance of power in many parts of the world, especially in the Middle East and the Baltic region, the outlook for the future may not be hopeless but it certainly looks bleak. The question is whether the brinkmanship of power politics and its potentially dangerous consequences will trump the diplomatic patience and resilience of those who are committed to a global democratic future. In order to get some added perspective, let us reflect on what we can learn from history.

29. Waller R. Newell, author of *Tyrants: A History of Power, Injustice, and Terror*, comparing Donald Trump to fascist rulers of the past. *Cambridgeblog.org* July 5, 2016.

Totalitarian Nationalism

Reflecting back on the traumatic history of Europe, Karl Jaspers, the German philosopher who had lived through the Nazi period, wrote his seminal book in 1949 on *The Origin and Goal of History*.[30] In it he spoke of an Axial Age, that defining moment in history when the major world religious traditions emerged which, many of us believe, help us understand our own times and what kind of human beings we are meant to be. With this in mind, the German sociologist Hans Joas has applied Jaspers's insights to some of the key issues now facing us.[31] In doing so he reminds us that totalitarian societies evolved in the ancient world along with the sacralization of power. Pharaohs and emperors not only ruled by divine right, they were regarded as divine with the power of life and death over their subjects. It was only during the global Axial Age, between 800 and 300 BCE, when prophets arose to challenge them on the basis of a transcendent power, that the divine pretensions of rulers began to be desacralized.

At the same time ethnic groups that claimed to be God's "chosen people," and therefore destined to rule the world, were also challenged. This did not mean

---

30. Karl Jaspers, *The Origin and Goal of History* (London: Routledge, 2010).
31. Hans Joas, "Sacralization and Desacralization: Political Domination and Religious Interpretation," *Journal of the Society of Christian Ethics* 36, no. 2 (2016): 25–42.

the end of such pretentious claims, but the beginning of what has become the perennial tension between attempts to sacralize nations on the basis of some ontological claim, and the prophetic rejection of such hubris. The Hebrew prophets regarded Israel as a "chosen people," but chosen to serve not just its own interests, but that of others as well. A "chosen people," says Jonathan Sacks, is "not a master race"[32]—an important message for the modern state of Israel, which has in many ways become a surrogate of the United States. The fact is, alongside belief in God, nationalism often makes the nation an "object of trust and loyalty,"[33] and God, insofar as God is part of the cultural equation, becomes a "mere name" to justify whatever the nation decides to do.

National identities and nation-states, we must always remember, are relatively modern constructions following the taming or eliminating of tribal authorities and loyalties, and imposing a new order, ideology, and set of symbols.[34] This would not be possible, of course, unless there was already some shared sentiment and system of values, the acceptance of a dominant language, a willingness, however lukewarm, to be part of the emerging nation, and a respect for its institutions. But tribal loyalties remain even when nation-

32. See Sacks, *Not in God's Name*, 198.
33. H. Richard Niebuhr, *Radical Monotheism and Western Culture* (New York: Harper & Row, 1960), 26.
34. E. J. Hobsbawm, *Nations and Nationalism Since 1780: Programme, Myth, Reality* (Cambridge: Cambridge University Press, 1992), 199.

alism reigns. Tribalism is, in fact, a potent expression of local interests and loyalties both within a nation and within global society, however latent it may be. As such it is a potential source of disruption and even revolt. To disparage the perceived needs and genuine concerns of tribes inevitably leads to protest and to the hardening of tribal loyalties. Trumpism marks the resurgence of tribal politics, but doing so by harnessing local and ethnic loyalties and interests to control a national agenda. In so doing, nationalism becomes exclusive rather than inclusive, a bulwark against the pluralist embrace of the "other."

The substance of nationalism thus varies from one context to another. Afrikaner nationalism in South Africa was Protestant, patriarchal, authoritarian, and ethnically exclusive. By contrast the nationalism embodied in the post-apartheid South African Constitution of 1996 is remarkably democratic and inclusive in its scope. Nationalism is therefore not always "right-wing" in character. You can be proudly American, German, Indian, or South African, and therefore genuinely patriotic, without being a right-wing nationalist who rejects pluralism. A key difference is that right-wing nationalism makes absolute, ontological, or God-given claims, and therefore demands uncritical allegiance from citizens. It is totalitarian, brooking no dissent. But such claims have no rational or historical basis; they are the product of political hubris and fantasy in the interests of gaining legitimacy and loyalty. They are ideological constructs used to justify national agendas and control power-relations in the interests of those who have gained power whether legitimately or not. And what is more, Hans Joas has noted:

> In the totalitarianisms of the twentieth century . . . we find forms of the self-sacralization of the state and of political leaders of a magnitude that recalls the archaic state, but now intensified beyond measure through the technological means now available.[35]

Some date the rise of right-wing nationalism in the modern era to the influential *Addresses to the German Nation* given in 1807–8 by the philosopher Johann Gottlieb Fichte, who argued that Germany had a special destiny to dominate the world because of its racial purity and cultural superiority.[36] This provided the ideological basis for both rabid anti-Semitism and the establishment of the Second German Reich after the defeat of France by Prussia in 1871 under Kaiser Wilhelm I and General Otto von Bismarck, which, said the general, "resembles God's creation of the world!"[37]

Bismarck, not Hitler, I suggest, is the prototype of Trump. Consider the words of contemporary historian Margaret MacMillan: "Otto von Bismarck had an outsized personality which would have sent waves

---

35. Joas, "Sacralization and Desacralization," 38.
36. Gregory Moore, ed., *Fichte: Addresses to the German Nation*, trans. and ed. Gregory Moore (Cambridge: Cambridge University Press, 2008).
37. Emil Ludwig, *Bismarck: The Story of a Fighter* (London: George Allen & Unwin, 1927), 253.

through whatever society he found himself in, but he was fortunate, even if much of Europe wasn't, that fate gave him a big stage to act on."[38] Bismarck, who loved to strut around in flamboyant uniforms, was no soldier, but he dominated German and European politics in his generation, and what is more, although claiming to be a Christian, he did not believe in forgiveness, "lied without hesitation and invariably blamed others for his mistakes."[39] The importance of this comparative aside will be become clearer in chapter 4 when we reflect on the leaders we need to take us into the future.

For now, let us turn the clock back from Bismarck and the foundation of the German nation to the American Revolution (1763–1787), which led thirteen former British Colonies to create a new nation, and do so with the same Bismarckean conviction that Divine Providence was at work. Some of the present conflicts in America are already evident back then, as can be seen in the disagreements between John Adams, the second president of the United States, and Thomas Jefferson, who succeeded him, both of whom had a hand in drafting the Constitution, and in preparing the stage for the later cleavage between Democrats and Republicans. In fact, Jefferson acknowledged that the Constitution was not just when it came to the position of slaves but, as

38. Margaret MacMillan, *History's People: Personalities and the Past* (London: Profile Books, 2015), 10.
39. Ibid., 16.

one of his critics declared at the time, Jefferson tried to put a good construct on the matter because it was vital to Jefferson "that he make everything America did seem good."[40]

The truth is, the United States was essentially a European nation transplanted into the New World comprised of the descendants of early settlers and millions of others of different ethnic origins, many of them religious dissenters, poor and unskilled, who emigrated to the United States during the later eighteenth and nineteenth century.[41] There was no intention or will to include either the Native Americans, whose land was expropriated by conquest and treaty or, on the part of most, the slaves brought from Africa to provide labor. The United States, it was generally agreed, had been an act of providence with a "manifest destiny" as a white, Protestant nation. Less than a century later it became clear that the fundamental disagreements entrenched in American culture around slavery and citizenship had not been resolved. The Civil War (1861–1865), often regarded as the bloodiest in American history, was a war among European colonists about the kind of nation America should become. That war continues in the political struggles

40. Henry Wiencek, *Master of the Mountain: Thomas Jefferson and His Slaves* (New York: Farrar, Straus & Giroux, 2012), 67; David McCullough, *John Adams* (New York: Simon & Schuster, 2001), 374–81.

41. See Roland H. Bainton, *Christian Attitudes Towards War and Peace: A Historical Survey and Critical Re-evaluation* (Nashville: Abingdon, 1960), 190.

that have continued ever since, and never more so than today, even if by others means.

The same colonial process of European expansion and aggression, often with the same lofty divine justification, took place in Australasia and in southern Africa to mention but two other British colonies. Colonialism was not only a symbol of national greatness among European nations, but colonies were also a place to send the unemployed, convicts, and others no longer needed, as well as a place from which to extract human resources, namely slaves, and raw material to feed the Industrial Revolution and increase national wealth.[42] As such, colonialism was a racist settler culture, which explains the persistence of racism and the later emergence of right-wing nationalism in the colonies such as Namibia, Australia, and South Africa.

The creation of the colonial nations in Africa was formalized at a conference convened by Bismarck in Berlin in 1884. It was there, without any African participation, that the continent was divided between the imperial overlords, with arbitrary borders drawn with their interests in mind. As often happened in Europe itself, so in Africa, tribal identities were ignored if not suppressed and European languages imposed, with the result that borders would become a source of ongoing conflict. European legal systems and styles of government were also transplanted, amended, and designed to further colonial interests with or without the sup-

42. Edward W. Said, *Culture and Imperialism* (New York: Knopf, 1993).

27

port of indigenous peoples. There was no thought about planting democracy except in some limited form among settlers.

Colonial wars of conquest were brutal and often genocidal, finishing off what had begun during the slave trade. The details need not detain us, but it is important to remember the consequences, not just for the colonies themselves, but also for what transpired in Europe itself. Some historians regard the genocide of the Herero and Nama peoples during the German occupation in Namibia as a precursor of the Holocaust in Nazi Germany. Likewise military tactics and weapons developed by Britain during the Anglo-Boer War in South Africa (1899–1902), essentially between two European nations, prepared for the bloodletting on the Western front in 1914. Concentration camps and the scorched-earth tactics employed by the British military were also a foretaste of what was yet to come across the Channel.

European imperial pride was insatiable, as was the desire to build bigger and better weapons, armies, and navies. Nations went helter-skelter in search of greatness. As Simon Winder describes it, colonial "gun-boat and machine-gun hysteria that racked so many places in the run up to the First World War formed a generalized European nadir, a sickness within much of the continent which would end up being turned on Europe itself."[43] So the way was prepared for the bloodletting

43. Simon Winder, *Germania* (London: Picador, 2010), 362.

on the Western front in a frenzy of jingoism, an extreme belligerent nationalism that had already emerged in Britain in its relations with Russia during the last decades of the nineteenth century.

> We don't want to fight but *by Jingo* if we do
> We've got the ships, we've got the men, we've got the money too
> We've fought the Bear before, and while we're Britons true
> The Russians shall not have Constantinople.[44]

A more immediate outcome of the Anglo-Boer War was the birth of a new European nation, the Union of South Africa, based on a racially segregated constitution approved by Westminster, which in turn paved the way for Apartheid. It was in opposition to this that the African National Congress was established in 1912, the first national liberation movement in colonial Africa. If European nationalism was forged by the Napoleonic Wars and those that followed between France and Prussia, African nationalism was born in response to colonialism and the struggle for liberation. This in itself gave nationalism a different flavor and ethos.

But whether in Europe or in the liberation struggles in the colonies, the attempt to change authoritarian or totalitarian nationalist regimes proved notoriously

44. A popular pub song written by G. W. Hunt during the war between Russia and Turkey in 1877–78. Jingo was coined to avoid using the name Jesus as an oath.

difficult given that colonial overlords, despots, demagogues, and oligarchies controlled all the instruments
of state security and power necessary to protect their
interests. That is why change usually came about, and
still does in such circumstances, by violent revolution,
tyrannicide, wars of liberation, or military coups. It
took Germany's defeat in the First World War, it must
be remembered, to end Prussian authoritarian rule
both in Germany and in Namibia.

Unfortunately the liberal democratic Weimar
Republic, which followed the defeat of Germany and
the abdication of the Kaiser in 1918, was a fragile
experiment in a newly constructed nation ill-prepared
for democracy. Germany was in dire straits. War veterans were divided in their loyalties, some leaning left
toward communism and others (Adolf Hitler among
them) to right-wing nationalism. The vindictive ter-
ritorial and financial reparations demanded by the
French at Versailles crippled the already-battered
economy even before the Great Depression wreaked
total havoc. In addition, Germany had no democratic
history, culture, or civil society; both the Catholic and
Protestant churches, as well as the military leadership,
were anti-democratic in ethos and supported the
return of the Kaiser from exile. Further, the democrat-
ically elected leadership had neither the confidence of
the majority nor the experience and power to manage
the country as it lurched from one crisis to the next.
The clamor for a strong, authoritarian leader grew

ever louder, not least among the younger generation, who felt betrayed by the failure of their elders.

The collapse of the Weimar Republic in 1930 provides a classic example of what has become a familiar sequence of events in postcolonial Africa, post–Cold War Eastern Europe, and post–Arab Spring Middle East. It is a sobering reminder of the fragility of liberal democracy in times when anger and despair undermine social cohesion, and right-wing nationalism becomes ascendant. A longing for a return to more autocratic and authoritarian rule is inevitable. So it is not surprising that many commentators have likened the resurgence of right-wing nationalism in Europe and in the United States today to scenes reminiscent of the rise of Nazism and Fascism, even if there are important differences that must be kept in mind. Even the United Kingdom, the bastion of political temperance and democratic government, has not been immune from such critical comment.

Following the British Brexit vote in June 2016, *Time* magazine devoted an issue to what the editor called "The Fall of Europe," and at least one columnist declared that Brexit heralded a return "to the grim 1930's for the liberal world order."[45] Whether or not this prognosis is accurate is another matter. But the question has to be asked: Will the EU survive as right-wing populism and nationalist sentiment increase across Europe, not least in France and Germany? There

45. Joe Klein, *Time*, July 11–18, 2016, p. 18.

is, after all, some legitimacy to the complaint that EU politicians sometimes ride roughshod over legitimate national concerns and too often act in undemocratic or at least overly bureaucratic ways.[46] But there is also a great deal of double-speak by opponents of the EU who criticize it for being elitist when they themselves are as elitist as anyone else, and sometimes more so. Of much greater concern should be the fear that the breakup of the EU might herald a return to conflict as the way to settle political and economic disagreement. The fact that NATO and Russia are increasing their battle-readiness does not bode well. It is sobering to remember that world wars in the last century had their origin in European squabbles, fears, and mistrust.

It is equally sobering to remember that it was only in 1992 that Eric Hobsbawm concluded that nationalism "is simply no longer the historical force it was in the era between the French Revolution and the end of imperialist colonialism after World War II."[47] Nationalism, he declared, was "past its peak."[48] The world back then had entered a new period of global international cooperation increasingly expressed through institutions and systems that transcended those of nation-states. The resurgence of right-wing nationalism and the apparent collapse of globalism,[49] along with the triumph of Trumpism and the march toward

46. See Das, *A Banquet of Consequences*, 251.

47. Hobsbawm, *Nations and Nationalism*, 169.

48. Ibid., 192.

49. John Ralston Saul, *The Collapse of Globalism* (London: Atlantic Books, 2005).

totalitarianism, indicate that Hobsbawm's obituary was dangerously misleading. And, as Thomas Merton, the prophetic-mystic, so passionately argued back in the 1960s, when it does it will embark on policies of hatred for the other and even war, encouraged by the mass media. He wrote:

> We have to consider that hate propaganda, and the consistent heckling of one government by another, has always inevitably led to violent conflict. We have to recognize the implications of voting for extremist politicians who promote policies of hate. . . .[50]

Keeping in mind the impact that the Great Depression had on Germany in fostering the rise of National Socialism, it is also important to remember that right-wing nationalism began to attract popular support in the United States following the banking crisis in 2007. Satyajit Das, who has documented its causes and consequences, speaks of it as "the most serious financial crisis since the Great Depression of the 1930's,"[51] and few countries have not been affected. It was the moment when the truth suddenly began to dawn on the average American and many other people that they had been living in a bubble of unreality, a dream world of unending prosperity that their children would also inherit. President Barack Obama came into office shortly after,

50. Thomas Merton, *Peace in the Post-Christian Era* (Maryknoll, NY: Orbis, 2004), 161–62.
51. Das, *A Banquet of Consequences*, 31.

with the task of dealing with the crisis for which he had not been responsible, but for which he would be held accountable by those who voted for Trump in 2016. Trump's election to fix the economy was one of the most far-reaching consequences of the Great Recession.

Racism, Islamophobia, sexism, and the rest, which found such horrible expression during the Trump campaign, would not have had the purchase they did if the American economy had not suffered in the way that it did. And the fact that the stock market did not collapse when Trump was elected certainly increased his supporters' certainty that they now had the leader who would recover lost prosperity and establish new jobs, rebuild industry and restore confidence in the "Rust Belt." The same was true in Britain when, following Brexit the economy seemed to strengthen, and those who voted out were vindicated, at least in the short term. It could, of course, be for longer. But we need to remember that the Germans who survived the Depression in the 1930s believed that Hitler had rescued their economy. The verdicts of history are long, not short term.

One of the ironies of the present rise of nationalism and the demise of globalism is the emergence of China as a champion of globalization.[52] This was evident when President Xi Jinping addressed the Davos Economic Forum in January 2017, and stressed the need to

52. See Žižek, *Living in the End Times*, 445–47.

build global economic policies and relationships. This is highly significant, because China is playing an increasingly significant global role, not least in Africa and developing economies. China is also the key partner within BRICS, an association of five nations, Brazil, Russia, India, China, and South Africa, representing half of the world's population with a combined GDP 16.6 trillion U.S. dollars, and a growth rate above average.

Whatever the weaknesses of BRICS and emerging markets more generally, developed and emerging markets need each other. How these relationships will be developed and managed now, given the resurgence of right-wing nationalism—or just nationalism itself—remains to be seen. But we must watch the space where Chinese and American interests collide as much if not more than where European interests are at stake. Hopefully, none of these growing tensions will lead to armed conflict or serious trade wars, but they are already affecting international efforts to deal with the critical issues affecting us all. Sampie Terreblanche, a leading South African economist, is also of the opinion that the "phenomenon of right-wing power" in the United States, rather than solving America's financial problems, may "turn out to be the Achilles heel of American financial power."[53]

53. Sampie Terreblanche, *Western Empires, Christianity, and the Inequalities Between the West and the Rest 1500-2010* (Johannesburg: Random House-Penguin, 2014), 499–500.

When South Africa decided in 2016 to withdraw from the International Court of Justice, there was, and rightly so, an outcry against the decision both within the country and within much of the international community. For the moment the withdrawal has been stalled by the Constitutional Court. Yet it is sometimes overlooked that the United States has never signed the protocol that led to the establishment of the Court, and Russia has also withdrawn. Such attitudes and actions are a consequence of the idea of national sovereignty, which allows nations and dictators to act with impunity in pursuing self-interested agendas. Most notably, this belief has scuppered many attempts to reach international agreement on nuclear disarmament, the environment, going to war, and the legality, for example, of the Israeli occupation of Palestine.

Politicians may espouse internationalism at summit gatherings, but they practice "fierce nationalism" in their practices back home.[54] All of this contributes to the political malaise that bedevils attempts to deal with the crises we face, undermining the ability of the United Nations to act timeously and adequately. The rise of right-wing nationalism exponentially exacerbates this isolationist tendency. With considerable foresight as far back as 1870, as nationalism was reaching fever pitch in Europe, the Swiss philosopher Henri-Frédéric Amiel remarked:

54. Das, *A Banquet of Consequences*, 6.

> It is strange to see how completely justice is forgotten in the presence of international struggles. Even the great majority of the spectators are no longer capable of judging except as their own personal tastes, dislikes, fears, desires, interests, or passions may dictate.[55]

In God We Trusted

In her novel *The Mandibles*, Lionel Shriver tells the story of an American family whose fortunes dramatically change when the country goes into financial decline in the second quarter of the twenty-first century.[56] The story is a futuristic parable of the decline and fall of the American Empire from the utopia of dreams to an "economic dystopia" that mirrored Germany in the Great Depression of the 1920s, as Shriver herself feared in writing the book.[57]

By 2029, the year the story begins, America is so heavily in debt to China that it cannot recover from the consequences of the banking crisis of 2007. The fortunes of an affluent white American family, the Mandibles, spanning three generations, are in sharp decline. China has become the greatest power on earth, the dollar has lost its value, and family inheritances are rapidly dwindling. Gradually the Mandible family has

---

55. Henri-Frédéric Amiel, *Amiel's Journal: The Journal Intime of Henri-Frédéric Amiel* (np. 2015), October 28, 1870, 169.
56. Lionel Shriver, *The Mandibles: A Family, 2029-2047* (London: HarperCollins, 2016).
57. In an interview with Stephanie Merritt on *The Guardian Books Podcast*, May 20, 2016.

to accept that the anticipated family fortune is gone. There is no longer a guaranteed comfortable future for the children or grandchildren of the family patriarch, let alone future generations, no medical aid to ensure good health treatment, or provide care for the frail and aged. Everything they had come to expect and felt entitled to have is gone.

There is no happy ending, but there are some intimations of redemption. Through all their trials and tribulations, some of the family learned hard lessons. Wealth had to be shared with those in need, caring for one another instead of being in competition was the only way to survive, and you are only entitled to what you work for fairly and honestly. In the process some Mandible survivors discovered the skills needed to negotiate the future, even a purpose in living. In fact, the process of living through the apocalypse was not unlike dealing with grief, from denial and anger through to depression and acceptance.[58]

In the concluding pages of *The Mandibles* news reports tell us that in 2057 Indonesia invaded Australia, a Palestinian State was finally declared, though nobody cared, and that Russia annexed Alaska for its natural gas resources, a step that prompted the Speaker of Congress to point out: "Alaska was always pretty far away anyway."[59] America had long lost the desire to police the world and control its resources. Maybe it

58. See Žižek, *Living in the End Times*, xi.
59. Shriver, *The Mandibles*, 401.

was beginning to recover its soul. Yet, neither religion nor the church feature in *The Mandibles*, or play a part in the redemption of the family. Except, that is, for the subtitle of the book placed on the cover beneath a reproduction of the once mighty dollar: "In God We Trusted." In the past there was every reason to express gratitude to the "God of our Fathers" on Thanksgiving Day, for they believed in divine providence and trusted God accordingly.

Ever since that earliest Thanksgiving Day, despite economic depressions and wars, there was, at least for the descendants of the colonizers and subsequent immigrants, a sense that God had blessed their nation with abundance, even if Native Americans or slaves and their descendants did not share the same sentiment. But for the rest, trust in God and in prosperity were conjoined, or as Shriver puts it, economics had become America's religion, and trust in the dollar a "belief system."[60] So much so, that eventually faith in God was no longer necessary except as social convention and political requirement. The dollar had usurped the place of God, and the "prosperity gospel" replaced the good news of God's kingdom. The obligatory mantra "God bless America" was perfunctory at best, if used at all.

The fall of the American Empire, like that of all empires, has not yet happened. It is not yet 2029, but the year of Trump's inauguration when, for his sup

60. *Guardian Podcast.*

porters, God was never more alive and well than in the United States. God is great, like America is becoming again. The value of the dollar has not collapsed, and America has enormous resources of wealth, skill, and the knowledge needed to survive. Whatever adverse signs, it is still a place that many find attractive. Moreover, Trump has indicated that he will defend Christianity, and make America a safe haven for those Christians who are persecuted for their faith in Muslim lands. The truth is, Trump would not have won if he had declared himself to be an atheist, as some French presidents do, perhaps in an unguarded moment, nor would he have won unless he had considerable wealth.

The story of *The Mandibles* raises some theological questions for Christians, especially white and privileged ones whether or not they support Trump, or live in America. Does America, and the West more generally, have to go into decline in order to learn the fallacy of depending on privilege, whether as God's "chosen people" or nations of self-confidant secularists? Is faith in God contingent on sustaining the "American way of life" and its global equivalents at all costs? Are people who are different by virtue of their religion, ethnicity, gender, or sexual orientation, to be regarded as outside the blessing God bestows on some nations but not the rest? Is any nation divinely entitled to more than its fair share of the earth's resources? If stock markets crash, will faith in God dissipate as it did in much of Europe in the trenches of France? Is this a *kairos* moment for the West requiring the response of a prophetic theology? Maybe the rebirth of true faith is at hand, maybe the Second Coming is near. Maybe one day America will be both good and great again. It has the capacity.

Reflecting on developments in Europe in 1871 following the formation of the Second German Reich, Henri Amiel writing in his *Journal* noted the prevailing mood of fatalism, pessimism, and nihilism in Germany, and the shocking statement by the libertarian anarchist Pierre-Joseph Proudhon that "evil had become God." In response he wrote in the hope that this malaise would "bring back the mass of mankind to the Christian theodicy, to that hope in God which is neither optimist nor pessimist."[61] In a world where religious fundamentalism is in mortal combat with liberal secularism, where pessimism reigns and nihilism threatens, the question of God looms large.

The world has not gotten more peaceful as the new millennium proceeds, but more dangerous, and neither religion nor secularism has delivered on its promises. Trumpism is certainly not going to fulfill the deeper aspirations of the disenchanted. But is trust in God an option, not the God of Americanism but the God revealed in Jesus Christ? God was certainly invoked at Trump's inauguration to bless his tenure, even as many prayed to God to save them from the nightmare they feared. But are we believers in God deluded, as athe-

61. Amiel, *Journal*, December 29, 1871, p. 181.

ists insist, or worse, has evil become God as others charge? If not, who is this God and what on earth is God doing? What does it take to trust God again? Could it be that the end of the American dream and global white privilege is a precondition for the rebirth of faith, of humanity, and the recovery of soul?

2

Where on Earth Is God?

You are a God who hides himself.

—Isaiah the prophet[1]

Is any room left for God? Ask those who are anxious, and since they don't have an answer, they condemn the entire development that has brought them to this impasse . . . we cannot be honest unless we recognize that we have to live in the world—"etsi deus non daretur."

—Bonhoeffer[2]

---

1. Isa 45:15.
2. Dietrich Bonhoeffer, *Letters and Papers from Prison*, Dietrich Bonhoeffer

> No one can answer the theodicy question in this world, and no one can get rid of it. Life in this world means living with this open question and seeking the future in which the desire for God will be fulfilled, suffering will be overcome, and what has been lost will be restored. The question of theodicy is . . . the all-embracing eschatological question.
>
> —Jürgen Moltmann[3]

As members of the Volmoed Community, Isobel and I participate every day in morning prayer for the needs of the world and for people who are suffering from illness, loss, and grief. But I often ask myself: Can prayer stop cancer from spreading, bring rain in times of drought, save a child from drowning, bring justice and liberation to the oppressed? On hearing about yet another death of an innocent victim, a doctor friend looked me in the eye across the dinner table and asked: What does the theologian have to say? Those skeptical about Christian faith and hope often start their critique by asking the same, and people of faith are by no means immune to doubt. Why do good people too often die young, and cruel dictators wield power so long? Why do we elect misleaders to high office? As Desmond Tutu once said, "God is often God's worst enemy!"[4]

Works, vol. 8, ed. John W. de Gruchy (Minneapolis: Fortress Press, 2010), 478—"as if God did not exist."

3. Jürgen Moltmann, The Trinity and the Kingdom, ed. Margaret Kohl (Minneapolis: Fortress Press, 1981), 49.
4. Desmond Tutu, "God Is God's Worst Enemy," in Living on the Edge: Essays in

The book of Job reminds us that this theodicy problem lies at the heart of the journey of faith. Job is a god-fearing man, but, says Satan as he enters into a wager with God, this is only because God has blessed him so much. In order to settle the bet God causes Job to lose everything he has, children and possessions, and he is covered with leprous sores. His wife is so angry with God that she tells Job to curse God and die. Friends come to provide counsel and comfort. They sit alongside him for seven days and nights before opening their mouths, listening to what has befallen their friend. Their responses are thoughtful, conventional wisdom at its best, even convincing at times.[5] They present their case with skill and consideration, trying to be helpful. But the bottom line is clear. Job must have done something very wrong to deserve his fate. If we keep God's commandments, we flourish; if we disobey, we suffer. Job pleads his innocence. His friends' arguments do not stand up to the critical scrutiny of his lived experience. He has done nothing to deserve what God has done to him. Either he is kidding himself, or else God is not the God in whom he had put his trust.

The questions are stark: How dare we speak about God as just and loving in the face of the abysmal narrative of global suffering?[6] How come despots are allowed to play poker with the fate of the world and

Honour of Steve de Gruchy, ed. James R. Cochrane, Elias Bongmba, Isabel Phiri, and Des van der Water (Pietermaritzburg, South Africa: Cluster, 2012), x–xv.

5. Walter Brueggemann, *Theology of the Old Testament: Testimony, Dispute, Advocacy* (Minneapolis: Fortress Press, 1997), 387.

45

put countless lives at risk? Theologians know that the theodicy problem is where faith in God is most vulnerable, contradicted too often by experience. Can we only expect to find answers when "the end" arrives and all is revealed, or does some light shine through the cracks in the meantime to sustain faith, as Leonard Cohen might have said?

The Achilles Heel of Theology

When Jesus spoke about "the end" he highlighted two signs that would herald his Second Coming: natural catastrophes ("acts of God" according to insurance agents), and those caused by us humans ourselves, such as war. These occur with such regularity that those who have expected "the end" during their lifetime can be excused for thinking that it is always imminent despite repeated disappointments.

But why should disasters that cause such havoc and suffering be regarded as signs of the coming of God's kingdom of healing, justice, and peace? Is God the agent of natural disaster and a God of war who condones violence if it serves God's purpose? Is Armageddon part of the divine plan? Is this really what God wills in order to establish peace on earth? Can the end justify the means God uses any more than it can justify what we do? Did God get Judas to betray Jesus? If not,

6. Johann Baptist Metz, *A Passion for God: The Mystical-Political Dimension of Christianity*, trans. H. Matthew Ashley (Mahwah, NJ: Paulist, 1989), 55.

what on earth is God up to, if God "exists" at all? No wonder Jesus asked whether he would find faith on earth when he returned![7] Such faith is a precious commodity.

Already in the second century of the Christian era, apologists for the Christian faith had to respond to such probing questions posed by their opponents, not just unbelieving skeptics among the Greek and Roman philosophers, but also the spiritually informed Gnostics, Manicheans, and Zoroastrians. The latter were all dualists believing that there are two powers of equal strength in conflict with each other in the world, the powers of good and evil. The power of evil, not God, is responsible for natural disasters, wars, and suffering. The good God cannot be held responsible, for that is contrary to God's nature. The spiritual, which is good, and the material, which is bad, are in a state of constant warfare.

The theodicy problem is not one that bothers such dualists, but neither is it of great concern to atheists, deists, pantheists, Buddhists, or traditional African religionists.[8] It is only a problem for those of us who believe that God is the ultimate power in the universe, that God created all things good, and that God is also all-loving. For given these convictions, how do we explain evil and suffering? Does God will to prevent

7. Luke 18:8.
8. B. E. Oguah, "African and Western Philosophy," in *African Philosophy: An Introduction*, ed. Richard A. Wright (Lanham, MD: Rowman & Littlefield, 1998), 217–18.

evil, but can't? Then he is not Almighty. Or can God prevent evil and suffering, but does not want to? Then he is neither a God of justice nor love.

In his classic study, *Evil and the God of Love*, John Hick describes two distinct trajectories in the treatment of theodicy in Christian tradition. The one derives from Irenaeus, the second-century martyred bishop of Lyon;[9] the other from Augustine, the fourth-century bishop of Hippo in North Africa.[10] The Irenaean approach became characteristic of Eastern Christianity, whereas the Augustinian was the fountainhead of theodicy in the West. I tend towards Irenaeus's position, which is teleological in character, seeking to understand theodicy in terms of "the end." In his final days in prison before he was executed by the Gestapo, Bonhoeffer expresses his appreciation for Irenaeus' understanding, believing that "in the end" all things will be restored in Christ within the life of God, so that God is all in all.[11]

While both streams, the Irenaean and the Augustinian, contribute to the Christian response to the problem, Augustine's approach has undoubtedly had the most influence. A Manichean in his younger years, Augustine delayed becoming a Christian precisely because he could not reconcile the all-pervasive evil in the world with the goodness of God as creator. But

9. John Hick, *Evil and the Love of God* (London: Macmillan Fontana, 1968), 217–21.
10. Ibid., 43–95.
11. 1 Cor 15:28. Bonhoeffer, *Letters and Papers from Prison*, 230.

eventually he was convinced of the goodness and beauty of creation, and concluded that evil is the absence of both and ultimately powerless, and that God can and will bring good out of evil and suffering. These convictions are expressed in his *Confessions* and the *City of God*, written while the Roman Empire was crumbling before the Vandal invaders from Central Europe, some of them non-Catholic Christians. What on earth was God up to? The theodicy problem was not only about personal suffering or natural disasters, it was also about the collapse of nations and empires, and the failure to achieve justice and maintain peace.

Since many believed that the Roman Empire, which had espoused Christianity as its official religion, was protected by God's providence and divinely appointed emperors, and that the *pax Romana* was necessary for the spread of the gospel, Augustine knew that the fall of the empire was a catastrophe that threatened to undermine social stability and even faith in the Christian God. But he also knew that the reason for the collapse of the empire was the greed, corruption, and arrogance of Rome, its endless wars, political infighting, and the failure of justice. The "wrath of God," as the Hebrew prophets knew, was a metaphor for the inevitable outcome of such human disobedience. Faith in God, Augustine argued, is not dependent on the prosperity of the empire, but on seeking God's kingdom and justice above all else.[12] Don't blame God for the fall of the empire, you Romans, Augustine was saying, blame yourselves. You get the Caesars you deserve. It is a warning to all that empires fall, not because they are attacked by enemies, but because of their own stupidity and folly, their moral failure and lack of good leaders.

Augustine's theodicy remained largely unchallenged through to the seventeenth century when, during the English Civil War as apocalyptic fervor flourished, the Puritan poet John Milton wrote *Paradise Lost* in order to "justify the ways of God to men."[13] Like Augustine, for Milton and his Puritan contemporaries, the sovereignty of God was the cornerstone of faith in God, Adam's "Fall" the clue to understanding both personal and political evil, and the Providence of God the basis for perseverance. And central to the doctrine of God's sovereignty was God's eternal decrees whereby some are elected to salvation and others condemned to damnation. As long as these dogmas held, Christians knew that faith in Christ could triumph over any adversity and they would regain the paradise they had lost in Adam.

Paradise Lost ranks high in the canon of Western literature but it is bad theology lacking the profound depth, Trinitarian subtlety, and Christological focus to be found in Augustine. Milton's portrayals of Satan and the origin of evil are convincing enough, but not his

12. See Hans von Campenhausen, "Augustine and the Fall of Rome," in *Tradition and Life in the Church* (London: Collins, 1968), 201–16.

13. Harold Bloom, *The Western Canon* (London: Harcourt, Brace and Co., 1994), 170–75.

portrait of God, which raises more questions than providing answers. If you can only fear or, like Job's wife, hate God as unfair Judge, but not love God as compassionate Redeemer, God has no beauty to attract devotion, even if there are other reasons to believe. If Judas betrayed Jesus because this was the foreordained will of God, then God was guilty, not Judas, for Judas's hands were tied. Sadly, it is Milton's theology that prevails in contemporary fundamentalism.

The theodicy problem refused to go away, but it was only by the end of Milton's century that the Enlightenment philosopher Leibniz gave it its name, and tried to solve the problem on the basis of reason rather than faith. With an optimism that reflected the confidence of the age, but not the realism of the Bible or that of Augustine and Julian of Norwich, Leibniz believed that all was well with the world. It ran like a well-made clock set in motion by an all-wise and benevolent Creator. Human progress was assured, as was the taming of nature. But just when all seemed well, sufficient to justify Leibniz's encouraging philosophy, the scientific doctrine of inevitable progress that was coming into vogue, disaster struck.

"Acts of God" and Human Folly

On All Saints' Day, November 1755, a massive earthquake flattened Lisbon, the capital city of Portugal. Eighty-five percent of the buildings in the city were destroyed, including all the churches. Thousands of worshipers perished, having gathered to celebrate the annual festival when Christians remember the faithful departed. Those left behind were not only in a state of shock but also devastated by the fact that the God they trusted had failed to protect even those praying to him at that fateful hour. If this was God's punishment for civic immorality, as some preachers claimed, why, people asked, were the churches destroyed and the red-light district left unscathed? Or is a caring, compassionate God another of the confabulations we create when reality becomes more than we can manage? If so, then we humans are on our own, up the proverbial creek, as we seek ways to deal with the crises of our time and face the approaching end.

What happened that fateful day in Lisbon has become, so it seems, a more frequent happening these days, adding greatly to global apocalyptic anxiety. Isobel and I were in Norcia (Nursia), Italy, the birthplace of St. Benedict, the founder of Western monasticism, deep in the Apennines, three months before the nearby village of Amatrice was destroyed by a powerful earthquake in August 2015. Nowhere seemed safer and more secure than that beautiful region as we traveled through, stopping to enjoy its sights and culinary delights. But suddenly, during that night in August, the earth opened up, hundreds of people were killed, and many more injured beneath the rubble. Some were taken, some left behind.

On that same day a thousand people were killed by Hurricane Matthew in Haiti. Then, a few weeks later, a devastating earthquake struck Norcia itself, reducing the ancient basilica dedicated to St. Benedict to rubble. Not long after, yet another earthquake struck Christchurch on the east coast of New Zealand, the second in a few years. The first had virtually destroyed the Anglican Cathedral in the city center; the second was no less threatening in effect if not in actual damage. People across the Pacific Rim, from Alaska to Japan, wait in trepidation for the next tsunami or quake to strike, precipitated perhaps by the failure of one of the many nuclear power stations that increasingly dot the landscape.

We do not need much imagination to visualize the scenes accompanying these disasters, for within minutes we watch them play out on television, albeit from a safe distance. But the sight and sound of the anguished cry of a mother who had lost a child in Amatrice remains implanted in my mind: "Where is God?" It is a cry that echoes through history, as it does through the pages of the Bible. Read the Psalms or the Book of Lamentations, listen to Job in his desolation, or Jesus's cry of dereliction from the cross. It was my own cry on the day our son Steve drowned in a swollen river in the Drakensburg in February 2010. It is the cry of millions every day across the world. The theodicy problem is a cry from deep within the human heart.

Prior to the Lisbon earthquake in 1755, the Parisian

philosopher Voltaire had been attracted to the enlightened deistic optimism of Leibniz. But in the wake of this tragedy he sarcastically attacked such optimism, notably in his novel *Candide* (1759), one of the most influential books of all time. Optimistic views of history are an illusion, he wrote, and, what is more, they undermine efforts to change the world. Voltaire went further in his scorn. To believe all is well is not only absurd, but theological arguments to justify God in a world of evil and suffering, especially when Christianity itself has blood on its hands, are dangerously ludicrous. Loud echoes of that critique resound to this day.

Following Voltaire's scathing attack, atheism, hitherto the creed of a handful of more radical Enlightenment thinkers, soon became the default position of bourgeois Western Europe, notwithstanding pockets of pious resistance and religious practice. For convention's sake many bourgeois citizens may have still attended Mass, but for all practical purposes God was not part of the equation when it came to taking account of their affairs in daily life. Nourished by rationalism, trusting in science, and convinced about the inevitability of progress, European elites were confident about the future of the world and their role in it. The earth was becoming more, not less, stable. The notion that it would come to an end was ludicrous. Apocalyptic passages in the Bible were demythologized by critical scholarship, and the most frightening Psalms, which spoke of God's wrath being expressed in violent acts of nature or the defeat of enemies, were qualified with a concluding refrain that things—not least the social order—would remain the same as it was in the beginning.

There is no easy rational solution to the theodicy problem. But a scientific-evolutionary understanding of the cosmos may help us understand something of the inevitability and even necessity of the tragic dimensions of life to which it refers. Cold comfort, you might say, but a perspective we need in order to remain sane even if not fully convinced that God is just and loving at the same time. Maybe it allows some light to filter through the cracks.

Life on earth has only become possible because of the way in which the universe has been constructed in the course of its evolution. Crudely put, without earthquakes and bacteria there would be no life. The miracle is that out of the furnace at the core of the earth, and despite instability, life has emerged and flourished. Put in more scientific terms, the "theory of emergence" informs us that evolution is a cosmic process of increasing levels of complexity that encompass reality.[14] South African theologian Klaus Nürnberger states the case eloquently:

> Without entropy, there would be no energy, thus no evolution; without causality, there would be no physical

14. Klaus Nürnberger, *Faith in Christ Today: Invitation to Systematic Theology*, vol. 2 (Pietermaritzburg, South Africa: Cluster, 2016), 319.

process; without death there would be no life; without brain functions, there would be no consciousness; without our decision-making capacity, there would be no freedom; without social structures and processes there would be no context for a functioning personhood.[15]

Unless you are a fundamentalist who rejects such scientific reasoning, this enables one to understand better natural catastrophes, disease, and death, as a necessary and inevitable part of life. God's power does not overrule the laws that make life possible in the first place. The laws of nature make adaptability possible, enhance life through beauty, and enable us to live life more fruitfully. Chaos is real, but it is not normative; creativity is.

But what about war? Why does God permit such terrifying events to plague the landscape of history? Why did God allow people to evolve in such a way that we abuse our freedom to wreak havoc? Or did God create us as puppets, unable to act altruistically but inclined to act badly?

In 1789 the French Revolution sent even greater shockwaves across the Continent than the Lisbon earthquake had done previously. Promising liberty, fraternity, and equality, an infant populist democracy collapsed three years later in a reign of terror that only came to an end with the rise of Napoleon and his totalitarian, chauvinist rule. Driven by French impe-

15. Ibid., 325.

rial ambitions, Europe became a battleground as Napoleon's armies conquered one country after another until they were halted on the Russian steppes, and finally destroyed at the Battle of Waterloo in June 1815 by a coalition of armies led by Britain and Prussia.

The Napoleonic era of imperial ambition and war set in motion or increased the tempo of movements for social and political change. Massive unemployment after the Battle of Waterloo, especially in Britain, was partly "solved" by settling people in distant colonies, as happened in southern Africa in 1820 when the first major cohort of British settlers landed in the Cape Colony. The Napoleonic era had a further consequence. It accelerated the Industrial Revolution, not least through the demand for new weapons of war. Thousands of farm laborers, no longer needed as army conscripts, were uprooted from the land and forced to live and work in unhealthy conditions in mines and factories, laboring long hours for a pittance.

The rise of a strong bourgeoisie or middle class alongside this discontented working class led to further social tensions. In 1848 a series of democratic revolutions against the monarchies and aristocratic elites erupted across Europe, only to be crushed. Liberal democratic thinkers were disillusioned, while political conservatism and authoritarian rule flourished. The cult of Napoleon, whether in France or across the Continent, had given fresh impetus to establishing powerful nations under strong leaders. Prussia under Bismarck perfected the art of *Realpolitik*, which derived its values from Machiavelli rather than Thomas Aquinas, whose teaching on Christian virtue had previously played some restraining role in Western Christendom, even if not always heeded.

If the French Revolution was an attempt to establish a secular democratic society, the founding of Prussian Germany led to a militaristic and modernizing totalitarian state supported by the Catholic hierarchy and the established Protestant churches. The deeply entrenched view, reinforced by a distorted reading of Martin Luther's "two kingdoms" teaching, that church and state operated in separate spheres, meant that uncritical patriotism and blind obedience became esteemed Christian virtues. At the same time, the sovereignty of God provided the basis for authoritarian rule in God's name. Established Christianity whether in Germany, Britain, or elsewhere in Europe, regarded itself, and was so regarded by the state, as the bulwark against social revolution and liberal democratic rule. The stage was set for a new world order in which violent revolution and conservative reaction, fueled by conflicting ideologies confronted each other, shaping the future destiny of the Continent and by extension, European colonies across the globe.

Although wars of Napoleonic magnitude largely ceased and revolutions were soon crushed in the second half of the nineteenth century in Europe following the Franco-Prussian War, there was no peace in the newly founded European colonies. Peace at home simply provided time and space for fighting proxy wars in subduing native peoples, and in the process testing new weaponry. But, and here lies the rub, these brutal colonial wars not only killed thousands of people but, like all European wars whether at home or abroad, were justified in the name of God. They were necessary, so it was argued, as part of God's providential plan to spread Christian civilization. In fact, as General von Bernhardi wrote in *Germany and the Next War*, published in 1910, Germany not only had a right to wage war, but also a duty to do so. War, he said, was a "biological necessity," a law of nature essential to progress.[16] War had become an "act of God"!

When war finally broke out in Europe in 1914, men from the British upper classes, who as officers by birth had visions of glory, and masses from the working classes who were seduced by propaganda and would soon be slaughtered in the trenches, broke into cheers of acclamation as though God's kingdom was at hand. Ironically, both sides claimed God was on their side. War was needed to make Britain and Germany great. Statesmen who sought diplomatic solutions, and others who opposed the war, Christian pacifists among them, were scorned as unpatriotic. Jingoist military generals, some of whom had fought in the colonies, were applauded and given command, even though

16. See Barbara W. Tuchman, *The Guns of August* (London: Constable & Co., 1962), 25.

they were mostly unable to provide the sane leadership needed to prevent the slaughter.

Meanwhile chaplains in the trenches celebrated Holy Communion and buried the dead. But where was God on that God-forsaken battleground? Or in the military hospitals as casualties piled high? Or in the villages and towns caught in the crossfire? Or on the farmland and in the forests that were destroyed by artillery shells? When the church bells rang to announce the armistice, they sounded hollow. "A first-rate calamity to humanity like a European war," the Scottish theologian P. T. Forsyth wrote in 1917, "must create in many minds . . . a denial, of a God and Providence in the world."[17] But it was the poet Wilfred Owen, who was killed in action on the Western Front a week before the war ended, who more poignantly exposed the blind jingoism of those responsible for the butchery even as he praised the nobility of the soldiers who fought. No one better exposed the lie continually repeated by the leaders of warring nations: "It is sweet and right to die for one's country."[18]

Postwar developments ensured that the peace achieved, as much through exhaustion as anything else, was fragile at best but susceptible to either atheist communist control following the Russian Revolution

17. P. T. Forsyth, *The Justification of God: Lectures for War-Time on a Christian Theodicy* (London: Independent Press, 1948), 23.
18. Wilfred Owen, "Dulce et Decorum Est," in *The Norton Anthology of Poetry*, ed. Mary Jo Salter, Margaret Ferguson, and Jon Stallworthy, 4th edition (New York: W. W. Norton, 1970), 1276–77.

in 1917 or the resurgence of reactionary nationalist fervor supported by many Christians. This led in 1933 to the rise of Hitler and the Second World War, with the same prayers being offered in churches across Europe as well as in the colonies. And, of course, that war ended with the atomic obliteration of Hiroshima and Nagasaki, which, together with the Holocaust and atrocities without number, stretched theodicy beyond its limits. Since then we have had wars without end and uncontrollable attacks of terror justified in the name of God or Allah. The futility and absurdity of this continuing war of the gods, or the theological justification of violence in the name of God, is mindboggling. Has evil become God, as Proudhon said? Or perhaps God is dead and we have killed him, as Nietzsche declared around the same time.[19]

Is God Almighty or Love Unlimited?

Nietzsche knew that his devastating critique of the God of Christendom would not rid the world of the human longing for truth, goodness, and beauty, and therefore the ache for ultimate truth, goodness, and beauty, even if that could never be satisfied. This was not a cause for despair but for hope in the birth of a new humanity that would find meaning without God.[20] Belief in God

19. Friedrich Nietzsche, *The Gay Science*, ed. Bernard Williams (Cambridge: Cambridge University Press, 2001), 199.
20. Alistair Kee, *Nietzsche Against the Crucified* (London: SCM, 1999), 37–38.

was a stumbling block to human well-being and world peace, the same charge leveled against religion by the "new atheists" of our own day. But is the God they reject the God of Christian faith, or an idol that we create and manipulate in order to deal with our fears, insecurity, or will-to-power?

The outbreak of Christendom's suicidal First World War convinced some theologians of the truth of Nietzsche's iconoclastic critique.[21] Foremost among these was Karl Barth, a young Swiss pastor, who was appalled by the way in which Christianity surrendered its soul to German nationalism and gave uncritical support for Kaiser Wilhelm II's war. Christianity, reduced to middle-class religious morality, was incapable of responding to the eschatological apocalypse unfolding on the Western Front. In reaction, Barth did a theological somersault. He decisively broke with the liberal Protestant theology in which he had been nurtured, and rediscovered what he called "the strange new world of the Bible" which spoke of the radical Otherness of God and told us that we were living in the "end time." God was not the God of religion, nation, and culture, but the God who judges such idolatry, calling both church and nation to repent and pursue God's justice. Thus began a theological revolution without which there would have been no Bonhoeffer, no Barmen Declaration that challenged Nazi ideology, or Con-

21. See Friedrich Nietzsche, *Twilight of the Idols* and *The Anti-Christ*, trans. R. J. Hollingdale, introduction by Michael Tanner (London: Penguin, 1968), 22.

fessing Church that led the struggle against Hitler's nihilistic attempt to capture the soul of Germany.

It is important to revisit Barth's story today, not least to recall that his target in those terrible days of 1914 was "liberal" Christianity, which, he said, had lost the biblical plot. Some liberal theologians in America thought Barth sounded far too much like a fundamentalist in pronouncing God's judgment on the cultural captivity of liberal Christianity. But Barth was no fundamentalist; he was a prophet for his time. At least Bonhoeffer grasped what Barth had rediscovered in the Bible, and in the 1930s took his side in challenging the theological shallowness and cultural captivity of white mainline American Christianity.[22] The irony today is that it is Christian fundamentalism, which once was so countercultural, that has now become captive to Americanism. That is why Barth's radical prophetic critique of "culture Christianity" remains pertinent in these apocalyptic times. Those who believe that God is the god of war, nation, and ethnic exclusion, a god of arbitrary power, prone to human manipulation for our own ends, are breaking the First Commandment:

The struggle against such idolatry begins in the Bible itself, not just with regard to the idolatry of other nations, but also that of Israel. Otherwise the First

22. "The Theology of Crisis," Dietrich Bonhoeffer, *Barcelona, Berlin, America 1928-1931*, Dietrich Bonhoeffer Works, vol. 10, ed. Clifford J. Green (Minneapolis: Fortress Press, 2008), 462–76.

Commandment would not have been necessary in the Hebrew scriptures. Admittedly, the message is ambiguous at times, for God is often portrayed there as a God of war, the vengeful tribal God of Israel. It is precisely for this reason that the biblical literalism of Christian fundamentalism is so dangerous. You can justify horrendous crimes against humanity by quoting biblical texts or appealing to the sovereignty of God who elects some people and nations, and damns others. Yes, there are biblical texts that call for the stoning to death of adulterers and others that portray God as vengeful and violent. So it is pointless to try and reconcile the conflicting images of God in the Bible as fundamentalists do, for that is to miss the point of what is staring at us in the text. The Bible is documenting contending images of God, not trying to iron out their differences. There is a theological struggle going on in the text between conceptions of God as an all-powerful ruler who justifies all-powerful rulers and their surrogates, and the God who identifies with those who are oppressed and poor. The Hebrew Bible is, as Jonathan Sacks argues, "a national literature of self-criticism."[23]

Hitler, Barth reminded his students in 1946, had no difficulty in referring to God as "the Almighty." But, Barth insisted, God is not "*the* Almighty" unqualified. That is a false understanding of God's power. "The man who calls 'the Almighty' God," Barth said, "misses God

23. Jonathan Sacks, *Not in God's Name, Confronting Religious Violence* (New York: Schocken, 2015), 53.

in the most terrible way. For the 'Almighty' is bad, as 'power in itself' is bad. The 'Almighty' means Chaos, Evil, the Devil."[24] God is not a cosmic version of the "authoritarian personality" described by Theodor Adorno in the 1960s, the God who leads empires and nations into war and makes them great in battle. This is abundantly clear in Jesus's teaching when he reinterprets Scripture in ways that radically challenge those that take its prescriptions literally in a dehumanizing way and attribute them to God's will. That is "taking God's name in vain," which is a breach of the Second Commandment. When unqualified power becomes God, God becomes evil.

There is some truth in the charge connecting Abrahamic religion and violence,[25] but religion is not generally the cause of violence but misused for its legitimation; in fact secularism may be even more to blame. In any case, justifying violence in the name of God is for the Abrahamic faiths an act of desecration.[26] "War," wrote P. T. Forsyth, "is sin's apocalypse. It reveals the greatness and awfulness of evil, and corrects that light and easy conception of it which had come to mark culture and belittle redemption."[27] That is why Forsyth thought more highly of Nietzsche's critique of religious faith than that of other critics who were more

24. Karl Barth, *Dogmatics in Outline* (London: SCM, 1949), 48.
25. Sam Harris, *The End of Faith: Religion, Terror, and the Future of Reason* (New York: W. W. Norton, 2002).
26. Sacks, *Not in God's Name*, 103.
27. Forsyth, *The Justification of God*, 19.

rationalist and optimistic about human nature.[28] This leads us to a question that is complementary to the theodicy problem.

How is it possible to justify faith in *humanity*, in human goodness and rationality, in the will to work for the common good, in the optimism that drives progress, and above all, the hope that empowers working for justice and peace? The Enlightenment project has stalled along with the fall of Christendom; secularization has not solved the problems facing us despite its predictions about the gradual improvement of humanity. For Augustine, the fall of Rome was part of the human story that began with Adam's fall and Cain's murder of Abel. Taken literally, the fall of Adam can easily be decried as nonsense, but understood as myth it reveals profound albeit unwelcome truth about the abuse of our God-given freedom.

If anything, the war-narrative that begins with Cain killing his brother Abel and continues unabated in ever-extending circles, gives credence to Augustine's much-misunderstood doctrine of "original sin," which he developed as Rome collapsed into a pile of ruins. The truth in Augustine's doctrine is not that every child is conceived in sin, but that we are all subject to pride, power, and greed, which in turn traps every generation in a cycle of violent folly. The irony here is that Augustine's notion of "original sin," which has been scorned as antiquated nonsense by modernity, is

28. Ibid., 209–10.

not unrelated to the findings of modern genetics. "History repeats itself in part," so we are told,

> because the genome repeats itself. . . . The impulses, ambitions, fantasies, and desires that drive human history are, at least in part, encoded in the human genome. And human history has, in turn, selected genomes that carry these impulses, ambitions, fantasies, and desires.[29]

Our fate is not written in the stars or in God's predestined decrees. Human beings are not robots programmed to act in immutable ways. Alcoholics can stop drinking, habitual criminals can change their ways, and the human artisans of history can reject the genomes that lead to history repeating itself. Judas did not have to betray Jesus because God so ordained (that is theological rationalizing after the event), but because Jesus chose the way of the cross rather than the sword. So the debate about determinism and free will continues apace. Christian theology certainly acknowledges the genetically predictable, but is open to the surprises of grace and history, the belief that things need not stay the same or repeat themselves with an inevitability that assumes we are all trapped in an ironclad cage.

Theologically speaking, human freedom and contingency are not polar opposites, just as in God necessity and freedom co-inhere. "For God," writes Jürgen Molt-

29. Siddhartha Mukherjee, *The Gene: An Intimate History* (London: Bodley Head, 2016), 476.

mann, "it is axiomatic to love, for he cannot deny himself. For God it is axiomatic to love freely, for he is
God."[30] That is why, for Christians, the Trinitarian
understanding of God provides the way to respond to
the problem of theodicy, for within God the free creative power that brings the world into being and sustains it in being is united with the suffering love of God,
which is God's power operative in redemptive solidarity with the world.

From the beginning, Christian theologians believed
that the God revealed in Jesus the crucified Christ is
the same God whom Moses encountered at the burning
bush. This God is not one being among many others,
but Being itself, the origin and source of life in whom
we all "live, move and have our being." This God is
beyond our grasp and manipulation, that is, God is
"holy" but with us in Jesus Christ, sharing our humanity and suffering vicariously with and redemptively for
us. We know this, those first theologians said, because
the Spirit of God has bound us together within the life
of God. The word they used to describe this was *peri-
choresis*, which means "being in and for one another."[31]
God is One, but God is not a monad; God is a communion of distinct "persons" (not individuals) inseparable
from each other, a communion that draws us humans
into a relationship in which we do not lose our identity

---

30. Moltmann, *The Trinity and the Kingdom of God*, 107.
31. Catherine Mowry LaCugna, *God for Us: The Trinity and Christian Life* (San Francisco: HarperCollins, 1991), 270–78.

but discover who we are in relationship. This is what it means to "live, move and have our being" in God. It is precisely what it means to "love God and our neighbor as ourselves," for that is the nature of God.

The doctrine of the Trinity thus breaks with the idea of a static God remote from human experience and historical engagement, and instead speaks of a dynamic and creative Presence that draws us into a relationship of trust and love in company with others, a relationship that respects difference within the unity of Being. The full implications of this understanding of God only dawned after much reflection, marred at times by controversy and some hair-splitting attempts to express what it all meant. But nobody flinched from the debate because nobody thought that finding the words for the ultimate mystery of Love could be anything but full of paradox and ambiguity. The more the discussion developed, the more the mystery deepened. The outcome is the uniquely Christian Trinitarian "theology of the passion" that lies at the heart of the Christian response to the theodicy question.[32]

The Christian understanding of God is not, then, the God of Milton's *Paradise Lost*, the God of unbridled power, for God's will is creative and redemptive, and that means God's power is always qualified by love. God is not an omnipotent puppet master, a demagogue who keeps creation in bondage to a closed predetermined plan that does not allow space for creative inno-

32. See Moltmann, *The Trinity and the Kingdom of God*, 47–60.

69

vation generated by self-emptying love. In Forsyth's words: "God's love is the principle and *power* of all being. It is established in Christ everywhere and forever. Love so universal is also absolute and final. The world is his, whether in maelstrom or volcano."[33] Love is unlimited.

Reflecting on the role of lamentation in the Old Testament from this perspective, Catherine LaCugna observes that there are two approaches to the problem of theodicy and specifically the problem of human suffering. The reasoned approach, which regards suffering as forming character, or the result of free will, is calculated, she says, to "let God off the hook." God is not responsible for suffering and evil, even though God "creates the universe as it is."[34] The other strategy, she says, is to abandon both the questions and the search for answers as unmeaningful, and as in lament, "turn over our pain or loss or confusion to God." This, she says, "is the path of darkness and unknowing." It does not make suffering more intelligible, "but it establishes the proper context for grief and sorrow: the praise of God because of relationship with God."[35] But this journey into unknowing requires not only jettisoning images of God that are now seen to be idolatrous, but reimaging God and discovering with Bonhoeffer that it

33. Forsyth, *The Justification of God*, 166.
34. LaCugna, *God for Us*, 372n45.
35. Ibid.

is not an omnipotent God but "only a suffering God" that can help us.[36]

Rowan Williams, who was close by the World Trade Center in New York on September 11, 2001, later wrote in response about the danger of the imagination filling up "the void" with inadequate images of God, "when what we need is to learn how to live in the presence of the void."[37] God, as Bonhoeffer said, wants us to manage our lives before God as if he is not there.[38] This is a very disconcerting notion for many whose faith in God is contingent on God being a "very present help in time of trouble."[39] Yet it is unavoidable if we understand God's activity in the world in the light of the cross, when darkness covered its face. What Williams says has, in fact, a profoundly pastoral significance, for it helps us to see the need to live with the ambiguity of God's presence in God's absence, and thereby to move with Job beyond theodicy as a problem to participating in a journey into the mystery "in whom we live, move and have our being." It is only as we embark on that journey of faith that our questions cease in contemplative silence, and resurrection hope and even joy become possible.

Job's comforters, too, were finally reduced to silence, as silent as when they first arrived on the

36. Bonhoeffer, *Letters and Papers from Prison*, 480–82, 486, 501.
37. Rowan Williams, *Writing in the Dust: Reflections on 11th September and Its Aftermath* (London: Hodder & Stoughton, 2002), 11.
38. Bonhoeffer, *Letters and Papers from Prison*, 478.
39. Ps 46:1.

scene. Even the youthful interrogator who speaks last, and speaks the most sense, runs out of words. But it is not the silence of contemplation. It is the silence of the exhaustion that afflicts us all after a long argument in which both sides "know" all the answers and neither side will budge an inch—the exhaustion that follows an increasingly heated debate that leads nowhere. But this exhaustion sets the stage for the narrative to reach its climax. Job and God now continue the conversation, but it is no longer about God, rather it is with God, and though the exchange is sometimes heated and angry, it is intensely personal. But eventually Job, too, is reduced to silence. He too has run out of questions.

We have arrived back at the place where this book began. Questions, I wrote in the opening paragraph of the Prologue, draw us into a conversation to which there is no end. Doubts may never be extinguished, and therefore questions will persist. There is no rational solution to the theodicy problem, no neat theological response to the iniquity of suffering, to Auschwitz and Hiroshima, and countless crimes against humanity. We may believe that the theodicy question will be answered ultimately, but penultimately there is no resolution to the problem. On this issue like others, we "see in a mirror dimly."[40] Some theologians who wrestled with these issues in the 1960s, raised specifically by the Holocaust, discovered help in Shusaku Endo's

40. 1 Cor 13:12.

novel *Silence*, recently republished and turned into a movie under the direction of Martin Scorsese. Set in Japan in the seventeenth century, its background is the story of Jesuit missionaries and their converts who are persecuted for their faith and sometimes martyred. In particular the story is about Fr. Sebastian Rodrigues who, firm in his faith and set on martyrdom, ends up betraying Jesus like Judas. But paradoxically he does so, like Jesus, to save his flock from certain death. *Silence*, writes Scorsese in the foreword to the new edition, "is the story of a man who learns—so painfully—that God's love is more mysterious than he knows, that He leaves much more to the ways of men than we realize, and that he is always present—even in his silence."[41] It is then, when we too are reduced to silence, that the journey into mystery can begin in earnest. That journey began for me at the riverside where my son Steve drowned. In my grief I was not, at first, reduced to silence; quite the contrary, I uttered loud cries of grief. I furiously asked questions, and there are many times when I still do. But I was sitting where Job, his comforters, and multitudes of my fellow humans have sat, and I was finally reduced to silent tears.

Justice Is God's Public Love

The author, or perhaps the editors of the Book of Job,

41. Shusaku Endo, *Silence*, trans. William Johnston (London: Picador, 2015), ix.

tells us that it all worked out well in the end. But not all of us are convinced. Our lived experience tells us that our dead children do not come back to life, that those suffering from incurable disease do not regain their health, and that those whose land was dispossessed by colonialism do not have it restored a hundredfold. The truth is, at a personal level we may well be able to live with the pain that Job experienced, and in doing so may be led into the mystery of God's love. But what about God's justice in society? What about the restitution of land and the sharing of resources? No attempt to wrestle with the theodicy problem can ignore the fact that many oppressed people have lost faith in the justice of God—even though many others have found consolation in their faith.

To say that "God is love" means that God is present in the suffering of the world we inhabit in order to redeem and transform it. Or, to put it differently, the God who is love is the God who seeks justice. But determined by love, God's justice becomes restorative not punitive and coercive. This undermines all monarchical conceptions of God that give rise to false of notions of divine sovereignty that legitimize patriarchy and triumphalist crusades, individual self-interest, and totalitarianism. Instead it provides theological grounds for unity in diversity, equality in community (*koinonia*), and love expressed through justice and reconciliation. The rediscovery of how fundamental this Trinitarian understanding of God is, not just for speaking about

God, but also for Christian witness in public and political life, has been one of the major advances in theology during the past century.

Reflecting on Job's experience of God in the silence of his suffering, Walter Brueggemann observes that Israel experienced a *theodic crisis* once they settled in the Promised Land. Israel had suffered greatly from oppression in Egypt, but now all seemed to be working out for the good. God had blessed Israel and kept his part of the promise. The Deuteronomic covenant was intact. But the suffering of Israel at the hand of its enemies did not end, even when they struggled to be faithful to the covenant. God, so it seemed, had hidden himself, not kept his promise.[42]

Israel's exile in Babylon in particular thus raised fundamental questions not just about the faithlessness of Israel, but also about the faithfulness of God. If God loved Israel, why was Israel once again in bondage? What had Israel done to deserve this? Similarly, in the struggle against Apartheid, at every hero's funeral and protest rally, no one debated the existence of God, but everyone questioned God about what they had done to deserve what was happening:

Senzenina
Sono sethu ubumnyama
Sono sethu yinyaniso

42. Brueggemann, *Theology of the Old Testament*, 385.

Sibulawayo
Mayibuye i Africa.[43]

What have we done?
Our sin is that we are black
Our sin is the truth
They are killing us
Let Africa return.

Gustavo Gutiérrez spoke to this in his commentary on Job, where he says that for Latin Americans engaged in the struggle for justice the problem was not only how one can *do theology* after Auschwitz, as it has often been framed in post-Holocaust theology, but "to find the words with which to talk about God" today "in the midst of the starvation of millions, the humiliation of races regarded as inferior, discrimination against women, especially women who are poor. . . . What we must deal with," says Gutiérrez, is not the past but "a cruel present and a dark tunnel, with no apparent end."[44] What if, in the end, there is no justice?

The story of Job spoke directly into Israel's quandary in exile, requiring a fundamental shift in how God was understood. God was not a tribal deity, a national divinity. In fact God was continually "hiding himself" in the events of history, anointing pagan rulers like Cyrus, the Persian king, to be their messianic liberators

---

43. Zulu/Xhosa funeral and anti-Apartheid song.
44. Gustavo Gutiérrez, *On Job: God-Talk and the Suffering of the Innocent*, trans. M. O'Connell (Maryknoll, NY: Orbis, 1985), 102.

in one of the "great turning points in ancient history."[45] God was also no longer the chauvinist God of a "chosen people," but the universal and therefore inclusive God of all nations whose messianic servant brings "good news to the oppressed . . . binds up the brokenhearted . . . proclaims liberty to the captives and release to prisoners . . . and comforts those who mourn."[46] Precisely the task which, for Jesus, defines his own inclusive mission as the servant Messiah for Jew and Gentile alike.[47]

Let me bring this discussion to a conclusion, and prepare the way for part 2, by referring back to Bonhoeffer's distinction between the penultimate and ultimate. In the present time, as I said in the Prologue, we can never act with pure motives and intentions as though we had all the answers, or do so as if it is our task to establish God's reign on earth by whatever means here and now. Such radicalism, as Bonhoeffer calls it, "sees only the ultimate," and therefore disregards and breaks with the penultimate.[48] But the alternative is not the way of compromise, but acting responsibly here and now as courageously and concretely as we can, with "the end" of justice in sight within the constraints and possibilities of reality.

For Christians to say that they cannot participate

45. See Isaiah 45.
46. Isa 61:1–3.
47. Luke 4:14–19.
48. Bonhoeffer, *Ethics*, Dietrich Bonhoeffer Works, vol. 6, ed. Clifford J. Green (Minneapolis: Fortress Press, 2005), 153.

in political struggles for justice because they will "get their hands dirty" is a failure to act faithfully now with "the end" in mind. Likewise for politicians to say that when they enter parliament or congress they put aside their Christian convictions in order to engage in *Realpolitik* is untenable from a biblical point of view. But it would be equally problematic to try and resolve all conflicts by piously saying we must love our enemies as we might do in personal relationships. For love in political terms means justice, and loving one's enemy means treating those who oppose us with respect as persons, avoiding stereotypes that inflame hatred and lead to violence, and taking seriously those conventions that provide guidelines for the treatment of prisoners in war situations.[49] To set aside morality in situations of conflict means returning to the law of the jungle, surrendering our humanity, and denying our Christian faith.

How then do we live according to the Sermon on the Mount and participate at the same time in seeking to make this world a more just and peaceful habitat for all humanity? Do we have to withdraw from political engagement entirely or engage differently? Bonhoeffer's approach, which many of us seek to emulate, is the latter. We engage reality not by trying to bring about the ultimate, nor by compromising with the truth, but by participating in the light of the ultimate.

49. See Donald W. Shriver, *An Ethic for Enemies: Forgiveness in Politics* (New York: Oxford University Press, 1995).

Is this not what Jesus meant when he told his disciples to "strive first for the kingdom of God and his righteousness"?[50] How we should approach this within the given realities of contemporary politics where nationalism and authoritarian leadership threaten democratic justice and international peace, is the subject of part 2.

50. Matt 6:33.

PART II

The People We Need to Become

3

What Makes a Nation Great?

The trials and tribulations of the American republic have a way of setting the agenda for other democratic societies—for better or for worse, and no doubt some of both. The signs are not encouraging.

—Jean Bethke Elshtain[1]

South Africa belongs to all who live in it, black and white, and . . . no government can justly claim authority unless it is based on the will of the people . . . only a democratic state, based on the will of the people, can

---

1. Jean Bethke Elshtain, *Democracy on Trial* (New York: HarperCollins, 1995), 1.

secure their birthright without distinction of colour, race, sex or belief. . . .

—The Freedom Charter[2]

We cannot but behold our own face as it were in a glass in the person that is poor and despised . . . though he were the furthest stranger in the world. Let a Moor or a Barbarian come among us, and yet inasmuch as he is a human, he brings with him a looking glass wherein we may see that he is our brother and our neighbour.

—John Calvin[3]

In 1991, a few years before Hong Kong was politically reconnected to China, I met with a group of pastors in the city. One of them told me that he was about to emigrate to California. He anticipated that it would be very difficult to remain in Communist China as a Christian, so he was going to the United States to establish a base for his congregation, which would later join him there to live in freedom. Two critical questions came to mind as I listened to him. The first was whether it was more important for Christians to stay and witness to their faith where they were, rather than go to a country where Christians were by far in the majority and, ironically, sending missionaries to China? The

2. From the Preamble to the Freedom Charter approved by the ANC National Executive and adopted by the Congress of the People, Kliptown, Johannesburg, June 1955.
3. Sermon on Gal 6:9–1. Quoted in Eberhard Busch, "A General Overview of the Reception of Calvin's Social and Economic Thought," in *John Calvin Rediscovered*, ed. Edward Dommen and James D. Bratt (Louisville: Westminster John Knox, 2007), 75.

second was whether Christians had to live in a democracy, where religious liberty is upheld by law, in order to be Christian?

President Trump's decision to preference Christian refugees and "make America great again" reminded me of that conversation. He promises to make America wealthier, more secure and powerful, and "more Christian," as though Americanism and Christianity were the same. I did not hear him say he would make America more just, inclusive, and democratic. Quite the contrary, for his measure and model of greatness is the business empire over which he rules and his notion of Christianity is a mixture of the prosperity gospel, American culture, and the triumphalism of Christendom. I call this Americanism, the culture in which Trumpism thrives.

But is that really what constitutes national greatness? Obviously it is in the eyes of many, whether Americans or others, so if that is not the model of greatness, what is? What norms and measurements must we use? Must a nation be democratic in order to be great? Surely not, seeing that many nations have aspired to greatness, and some might be said to have achieved it, long before democracy was regarded as good political practice in the modern world. The popular and widespread notion of greatness measured in terms of power and wealth is nothing new. In the ancient world, the teaching of Israel's sages that "righteousness exalts a nation"[4] was exceptional, and remains so today. Yet that surely remains the template for any nation presumptuous enough to claim to be Christian, however rare it may be.

Most Christians have lived for almost twenty centuries in monarchical or totalitarian societies, and many have been persecuted for their faith even by so-called Christian rulers. So you do not have to live in a democracy in order to be a Christian, as my Hong Kong friends seemed to think, and you might be a better one if you did not. In fact, within a democracy the church is more likely to become a social club rather than a prophetic community. The ecumenical church in South Africa was, in some ways, more the church of Christ when it was engaged in struggling against Apartheid than it became after the new democratic era began. I have no doubt that democracy is more aligned with Christian social ethics than totalitarianism. But to be the church in a democracy demands spiritual resilience and a decisive prophetic commitment. And that requires an understanding of how best to participate in making a democracy more just for all, not just for some of the people.

There was a time when America was, for many of us, an icon of democracy, a country where freedom flourished, justice was pursued, and power shared. It was also the bastion of Christianity in a world becoming more secular. Americans, I learned from afar, believed they had a God-given mission to spread Christian val-

4. Prov 14:34.

ues, uphold human rights, spread, strengthen, and defend democracy across the globe. But I soon discovered this was only partly true at best; there was another "Christian" America, one that glories in its exceptionalism and divine mandate to control the world in its own interests. Fortunately a strong remnant remains of the Christian America I first knew. An American Christianity committed to the struggle for justice and human rights, a Christianity more inclusive in its vision, and one that in particular has taken deep root in the soil of African American culture.

The adherents of this more progressive Christianity perceive America's calling and greatness differently to that touted by advocates of Americanism. But they increasingly find themselves living in an alien empire like the early Christians, and are often reviled as unpatriotic and un-American. The historic parallel to this imperialistic America is not the Roman Empire of pagan times, or the British Empire that kept expanding its colonies, but the Holy Roman Empire of Christendom, the empire that Bismarck tried to resurrect, a Reich with its Dom built in Berlin to rival St. Peter's Basilica in Rome, and a Germanism that anticipated Americanism. Yet there is one fundamental and noteworthy difference between the American Empire of today and that of the Holy Roman Empire or Bismarck's Reich. That difference is democracy.

Democracy is a slippery term that means different things to different people. Just as it has become necessary in speaking about justice, to ask "whose justice?" are we speaking about, so it is necessary to ask "whose democracy?" are we talking about. In America, all Republicans and Democrats pledge to support the Constitution, but they often understand it differently. And these differences have far-reaching consequences, not only for Americans themselves but potentially for all of us. As Jean Bethke Elshtain, both a political scientist and a Bonhoeffer scholar, once remarked, democracy in America sets "the agenda for other democratic societies—for better or for worse" and went on to say that the "signs are not encouraging."[5] So answers to the questions whether democracy will survive in America, and whether it is able to provide the polity needed to respond responsibly to these apocalyptic times, have become urgent.

In 1941, writing about the future of Germany after the war, Bonhoeffer did not think that democracy would be feasible going forward, at least, not liberal democracy as practiced in Anglo-Saxon countries. Germans, he argued, were not prepared for democracy. What the country needed after years of Hitler and destruction was a strong government, and that was not provided by liberal democracy. But, he said, "this does not mean that we must continue to accept forms of state-absolutism."[6] The minimum necessary, he went

5. Elshtain, *Democracy on Trial*, 1.
6. Dietrich Bonhoeffer, *Conspiracy and Imprisonment: 1940-1945*, Dietrich Bonhoeffer Works, ed. Mark S. Brocker, vol. 16 (Minneapolis: Fortress Press, 2006), 536.

on to say, is a state limited by law and internationally recognized.

It may be true, as Waller Newell argues in his history of tyranny, that "enlightened despotism" can, on occasion, play a role in "laying the foundations for orderly, prosperous, and civilized societies." But this, he adds, is "the very best case scenario," a rare short-term exception.[7] In the medium and certainly the long term, there is no better alternative for human survival and achieving our greatest moral values than democracies that promote human freedom, tolerance, and cultural excellence. Tyrannies might restore order after civil strife, but they will soon turn corrupt and destroy the moral fibre of society.

The division of Germany after the Second World War into East and West—the one communist and totalitarian, the other democratic and capitalist—and the eventual collapse of East Germany, provides a textbook case of the strengths and weaknesses of the two political systems. But while former East Germans had grievances about the way in which they were absorbed into the West after reunification in 1990, and especially their loss of certain social benefits, few opposed the democratic Constitution of the new Federal Republic. Whatever its weaknesses, democracy was the best form of government available for building a just and equitable society, even if not perfect and in constant

7. Waller Newell, *Tyrants: a History of Power, Injustice, &* Terror, (Cambridge: Cambridge University Press, 2016), 231.

need of revision. This was not only a major advance in German political history, given its past preference for authoritarian governments, but the new Constitution was widely regarded as a model for democratic advance in the new millennium, something readily acknowledged by those who drafted the post-apartheid Constitution of the Republic of South Africa.[8]

What is also clear from this comparison is that there is not one model of democracy that fits all contexts. Democracy as it has developed in South Africa is not precisely the same as in Germany, and neither is the same as democracy in the United States, France, or Britain. Democracy is not a single polity frozen in time, and as such a commodity that can be exported from the West or anywhere else to other places. It is, rather, a hard-won struggle that has to be waged in every place until it becomes a way of being a nation rather than a political program that comes packaged with foreign aid ready for implementation. Like any fragile plant, democracy has to develop deep roots in the soil where it is meant to grow, and take on the character of that place so that it is owned and cherished. Failed states are invariably new democracies that have never had the time and resources to mature in context.

Unlike authoritarian regimes, which are virtually all alike, democracies, then, vary in emphasis and style from one historical context to the next. All true and

---

8. See Laurie Ackermann, *Human Dignity: Lodestar for Equality in South Africa* (Cape Town: Juta & Co., 2012).

just democracies today are clearly a far cry from their prototype in ancient Athens, where slaves and women were excluded from the vote. But democracy not only develops differently in different contexts, it is also a complex form of government, and always a work in progress guided by a set of values that are continually being expanded and contested. This requires a level of political maturity that has to be nurtured. But that does not mean that democracy has to be elitist. What it means is that unless a democratic culture develops in a country, democracy as a system of government will fail to achieve its goals, and there will be a hankering after an authoritarian government. Law and order generally wins over key democratic values, such as freedom and human rights, especially in times of political uncertainty and social chaos. So let us remind ourselves about what democracy really is, and how democracies can be nurtured and sustained.

Democracy: A Reminder

Democracy is government elected by and responsible to the citizens of a nation in free and fair elections. It requires the rule of law, promotes freedom, protects civil liberties, and insists on the separation of power between the legislative, the executive, and the judicial arms of government. But democracy has evolved differently in different historical contexts. In some it has developed within the framework of a constitutional monarchy, in others it is republican in character. In some, it is a secular humanist project, in others religion plays a significant role, and in others it coexists with an established church. But irrespective of the role of religion within it, democracy is not regarded as divinely imposed. It is an ongoing human construction guided by its founding principles contained in a constitution.

Despite these areas of fundamental agreement, democrats disagree on the extent to which personal liberties should be constrained by social responsibilities. This has led to the distinction between liberal and social democracy. There are also disagreements about the extent to which democracy should be populist, participatory, and representative. Populist democracy, which has its origin in tribal politics, encourages grassroots participation, but can degenerate into ill-informed mob rule. Even so, the active participation of citizens is necessary for a democracy to flourish, hence the need for a strong civil society. But the direct involvement of citizens in decision-making beyond the local level is often impractical. For that reason, representative democracy, whereby citizens elect others to act on their behalf, is necessary at least at regional and national levels.

Democracy has to be constitutional because it is dependent on the rule of law, not the whims of a monarch or president. This raises the question of the latter's place and role. William Everett, an American social ethicist, has noted an irony in the character of the American presidency compared with the British monarchy. Whereas the latter, which the American "Founding Fathers" rejected, now provides the cultural glue in an increasingly pluralistic Britain, Americans have allowed the office of the president to accrue "more and more symbolic power as the proper embodiment" of national "unity, ideals, and purposes." However, the president, unlike a constitutional monarch, cannot stand above the political fray and remain effective. Too often this tears "apart the bonds of civility, commonweal, and global leadership that have brought most Americans together since the mid-twentieth century."[9] The same problem has to be faced in all democracies, as in South Africa, where the president, who is meant to be for all, does not stand above party loyalties and conflicts but is embroiled in them. In Germany, which is a model worth emulating, the president is "above" party politics, while the chancellor is the leader of the governing party, the equivalent of the British prime minister. This was true in Germany until the death of President Hindenburg in 1934, after which Hitler assumed both roles when he became the Führer.

Unlike totalitarian and authoritarian societies, where everybody knows their place, in which roles are defined within controlled structures, and where order, efficiency, security, and centralized control are the norm, the situation in democracies is more fluid, var-

9. William Everett, "Queen and Constitution," blog posted on January 16, 2017.

ied, and sometimes messy. The rule of an absolute monarchy, a dictatorship, an elitist oligarchy of the wealthy led by a powerful president, is obviously not the same as the rule of law dependent on due process; nor are the decision-making processes of a parliament elected by the people for the people the same as those that occur when demagogues dictate. It is for this reason that democracies require a mature and informed civil society, a responsible but free media, and a legal system that is able to keep check on the way in which power is exercised. The most insidious enemies of democracy are propaganda, fake news, and the lie that undermines the constitution and allows power to be abused and become corrupt.

Democratic governments change through free and fair elections, but the transition from an authoritarian to a democratic order requires protest and pressure, and sometimes violence becomes inevitable. This means that such transitions are often disruptive if not chaotic, and the society that results sometimes takes years to reach a secure equilibrium if it ever does so. Spain after the Franco regime is a classic example. The same is true of many former Eastern European nations since the collapse of the Soviet Empire. This process of transition is often exacerbated by large-scale inequalities, a lack of resources, inadequate education, and the preparation necessary for democratic participation and ongoing transformation. Countries with a long democratic tradition are obviously better equipped than those that have recently undergone a transition from totalitarian regimes or colonial rule. The challenge facing "old democracies" is how to overcome apathy and fatigue in order keep the democratic spirit alive. One of the positives about the recent round of elections in America and Europe is that the issues have attracted more participation than is normally the case. In that respect, democracy is alive, even if not well.

Democracy is both a system of government and a vision of what a society should be and become. By democratic system I mean those constitutional principles and procedures, symbols and convictions, checks and balances, which have developed over the centuries in response to the broadening vision of a just and equitable society. But if we reduce democracy to a system only, then we fail to appreciate its character as an open-ended process shaped by a vision of a more just society. Democracy can then be frozen and co-opted to serve the interests of some, but not all citizens. The development of democracy is, for that reason, a constant struggle to extend and entrench civil rights, and promote human rights more generally. That is why it is sometimes said that democracy is a perpetual argument, something that is obvious if you watch proceedings in the British or South African parliaments as compared to a session of the Chinese People's Congress.

The sad truth is that people and governments might say they espouse democracy but only pay it lip service in pursuing their own tribal agendas. Tyranny may well arise, then, not just by overthrowing democracy, but under the guise of democracy through the control of wealthy oligarchies or political mandarins with insider knowledge. This has been labeled "totalitarian democracy," that is, the attempt to create a utopian society in which human rights and liberties are not controlled by the rule of law, but surrendered to the rule of an elite.[10] Corruption is inevitable. In times of crisis when, for example, refugees flood across borders putting democratic countries to the test, right-wing, anti-democratic forces are always lurking in the shadows waiting for an opportunity to take control. They know full well that people are especially fickle when their interests are at stake even in the best of times, but chronically so in the worst. So unless functioning well, a democracy can easily be captured by economic and political forces that determine who should be in power. This illustrates a sobering fact about the nature of democracy—it can regress, suffer setbacks, and in some instances it may not survive. In fact it can only endure if it encourages a strong civil society, and develops in more just and equitable ways. Which leads Newell to the important conclusion that for democracy to defeat tyranny, civil society has to "remain vigilant against the wolves who prowl the perimeter."[11] The

10. J. L. Talmon, *The Origins of Totalitarian Democracy* (London: Sphere Books, 1970); Karl Dietrich Bracher, *The German Dictatorship: The Origins, Structure and Consequences of National Socialism*, trans. Jean Steiberg (London: Penguin, 1973), 614–15.

perennial challenge is how to deal with the legitimate concerns of tribal politics without undermining democracy and resorting to violence or authoritarian forms of government, but in fact broadening and deepening democracy. The transition to democracy or sustaining it without ongoing democratic transformation leaves the system vulnerable, for it serves the interests of only some of the people.

Irrespective of the precise format that a democracy may adopt, it is respect for and the practice of democratic values that make a democratic nation great. Greatness, therefore, is not about size, military power and prowess, religious piety and liberty, sporting success, or the ability to dominate global trade and the strength of its economy. Democratic greatness has to do with freedom, justice, the way in which the vulnerable are treated, and the exercise of power for the welfare of all, including global society. When these values are subtly undermined or overtly attacked, democracy finds itself on trial and struggling to survive.

Democracy is also about the desacralization of power. A democracy cannot be other than a secular society, for if religion takes control then one of the pillars of democracy collapses, namely the freedom of religion, which also implies the freedom not to be religious. In this sense, there can be no Christian democratic nation, even though some nations may have a large Christian majority who influence its policies. Chris-

11. Newell, *Tyrants*, 232.

tians should therefore respect the secularity of the state as both theologically and politically necessary, but at the same time they have a responsibility to prevent secularism from becoming endemic.

By secularism I mean an ethos in which selfish individualism disregards and undermines the common good, and freedom becomes a license for destructive policies and behavior. But to make a nation great does not mean making it more Christian, Muslim, Jewish, Buddhist, or Hindu, but more just and equitable. For a president to be sworn into office with his or her hand on the Bible or its equivalent may satisfy some religious constituencies, but if it is an attempt to achieve some kind of divine legitimacy driven by the will-to-power and tribal interests rather than a commitment to serve an inclusive common good, it undermines democracy. What is far more important in a democracy is that the president promises to uphold the constitution. Democracy requires, then, the desacralization of power. Democracy is not a radical polity that seeks to bring in the millennium, whereas hegemonic power attempts to do precisely that, and too often in the name of God.

Power is like wealth: the more you have the more you want, and the more you are tempted to justify it. Such power usually entrenches itself through patronage, as it did in Germany among the increasingly prosperous bourgeoisie during the nineteenth century. And, now, writes Fred Dallmayr, "the prevailing inequalities of power, wealth, and knowledge coalesce today into a formidable pyramidal structure, that is, the structure of an unprecedented global hegemony."[12] To counter this powerful global force involves an unending struggle. This may mean making strategic compromises on some secondary issues, but it demands a great deal of courage, intellectual effort, and political wisdom to prevent such power from undermining the very essence of democracy itself.

The fact that democratic constitutions are sometimes amended is a good indication that democracy itself is a work in progress, and the fact that constitutional amendments are usually very contentious and seldom made without a fight, indicates that democracy is a site of struggle. So to claim that the American Constitution, for example, must be upheld in terms of what the original drafters intended, is misleading. After all, many of them were slave owners, so the question of slavery was fudged at the time The character of democracy as an ongoing struggle becomes obvious if we look back on its evolution in America.

Democracy as a Site of Struggle

In 1831 the French diplomat Alexis de Tocqueville visited the United States and, on the basis of his observations, wrote *Democracy in America.* De Tocqueville had

12. Fred Dallmayr, *Dialogue Among Civilizations: Some Exemplary Voices* (New York: Palgrave Macmillan, 2002), 81.

grown up at the end of the Napoleonic era and was well aware of the difficulty of establishing a democracy of liberty, equality, and fraternity in the wake of a Revolution, a Reign of Terror, and the rule of a despot, Napoleon. When he visited America, it had already successfully revolted against the British monarchy, and as a transplanted conglomerate of immigrants and refugees from Europe was trying to build a democratic republic under the combined, though sometimes contradictory, influence of Enlightenment philosophy guided by reason and Puritan theology guided by Scripture.

De Tocqueville was astonished to find that religion and authoritarianism, the major sources of conflict in Europe, were reconciled with enlightenment and freedom in America. "No religious doctrine," he wrote, "displays the slightest hostility to democratic and republican institutions."[13] He was also surprised to discover that Christian freedom was equated with democratic religious liberty. Democracy in America, he surmised, had a very good chance of success. But he warned about the danger of "soft despotism" in which presidents rule imperiously, and the "tyranny of the majority," in which the will of the people is manipulated even against their own good. He was echoing what Plato and others had said down the ages since the first democratic experiment in ancient Athens.

In assessing Tocqueville's report, we must remem-

13. Alexis de Tocqueville, *Democracy in America* (New York: Vantage, 1956).

ber that the America he visited was largely homogenous. The right to vote was restricted to white males who owned property, the vast majority of them Protestants. To keep America racially and religiously uniform was deemed prudent and necessary for the young democracy. For this reason, and to appropriate more land, the Indian Removal Act had just been passed, forcing Native Americans beyond the boundaries of colonial America. To make America prosperous, slavery was also regarded as necessary; but slaves by definition were not citizens. In fact they were often regarded as only two-thirds human. It would be another thirty-two years before the Emancipation Proclamation changed their legal status, and more than a century before some could vote. Women, whatever their color, did not qualify to vote, as was also the case throughout Europe. There was also no need to build a wall between the United States and Mexico to keep illegal immigrants out because Texas was only seized in 1845. But European immigrants were welcomed by the boatload, even if Jews and Catholics were regarded with suspicion. The fledgling nation had a long way to go before it could be deemed truly democratic or "great"; it also still had to be tested by a Civil War that was fought over the direction the young democracy should take into the future. American democracy, in sum, was an unfinished project. It was racist and patriarchal to the core. That has proved to be a huge legacy to overcome.

Nevertheless, De Tocqueville would be very surprised if he revisited America today. The "soft despotism" and the "tyranny of the majority" that he feared have, in fact, become a threat to democracy, religion has become a divisive political factor, and the descendants of the slaves have the vote though still, in places, struggle to exercise it. By comparison, in Western Europe relations between Catholics and Protestants have improved beyond all recognition due to secularization and the ecumenical movement, but religious and cultural tolerance in Europe is being tested as a result of Muslim immigration, religious extremism, and the resurgence of right-wing nationalism.

At the same time secularism has eroded the spiritual foundations that once provided the basis for European social cohesion. The demise of Christendom, for all its faults, has left a spiritual vacuum, something that Bonhoeffer and others anticipated.[14] A democracy may need to be secular, but it would be much the poorer without the insights and participation of faith communities that have learned to respect each other and understand their servant role in a democracy.

When Bonhoeffer, who has been labeled "a theological de Tocqueville,"[15] arrived in New York a century later, in 1930, as a visiting student at Union Theologi-

---

14. Bonhoeffer, *Letters and Papers from Prison*, Dietrich Bonhoeffer Works, vol. 8 (Minneapolis: Fortress Press, 2010), 500.

15. Ruth Zerner, "Dietrich Bonhoeffer's Views on the State and History," in *A Bonhoeffer Legacy: Essays in Understanding*, ed. A. J. Klassen (Grand Rapids: Eerdmans, 1981), 151.

cal Seminary, America was different. The Civil War had been fought, the slaves emancipated, and the United States had enlarged its continental territory by conquering bits of Mexico. It was in the process of moving from being a somewhat isolated republic to becoming the empire we now know. But America was still a lively democracy envied by European immigrants and refugees as the "home of the free," where initiative was handsomely rewarded and dreams realized, and you could worship God as you liked or not at all.

Bonhoeffer, eager to learn all he could about American society, was, like most Germans of the time, suspicious of democracy. He had left behind a democracy in tatters. By the end of 1929, the German people had lost all confidence in the Weimar Republic and its elected leaders, and had little faith in democratic institutions to weather the storm. Many believed the situation demanded *Realpolitik* led by a latter-day Bismarck to make the nation great again. To much public acclaim, the military dominated by Prussian generals tried to restore order, but actually fatally undermined parliamentary authority and made it possible for Hitler to seize power. As Klaus Fischer puts it: "Despite the fact that the Weimar Constitution had created the conditions for a parliamentary democracy, old habits of relying on authoritarian methods proved to be the stronger in the end."[16]

16. Klaus P. Fischer, *Nazi Germany: A New History* (New York: Continuum, 1998), 224.

Bonhoeffer's year in New York was life-changing. Under the influence of a French pastor and fellow student he jettisoned the last vestiges of his German nationalism and even embraced pacifism. He also became critical of the "white Christianity" of liberal Protestantism and embraced African American Christianity through his involvement in the Abyssinian Baptist Church in Harlem.[17] There he discovered a healthy blend between the evangelical gospel of salvation in Christ and the social gospel that advocated human rights in an effort to extend God's rule of justice. Black Christianity was a powerful indictment of white racism, whether in the blatantly racist southern fundamentalist churches, or the northern more liberal white churches, whose theology lacked evangelical depth and whose congregations remained almost as segregated as those in the South.

Bonhoeffer returned to America a second time in 1939. By now he had lived through the rise of Hitler in a Germany that was on the brink of going to war yet again. He had also reflected in greater depth on his earlier American experience. In the report he wrote, he compared the differences between democracy in France and the United States, which, he said, arose out of their respective Revolutions.[18] The first was anti-

17. See Josiah Ulysses Young III, *No Difference in the Fare: Dietrich Bonhoeffer and the Problem of Racism* (Grand Rapids: Eerdmans, 1998), 25–27.

18. Bonhoeffer, "Protestantism without Reformation," in *Theological Education Underground*, trans. Scott A. Moore, Dietrich Bonhoeffer Works, vol. 15 (Minneapolis: Fortress Press, 2011), 438–62.

Christian in character, and led to a secular state in which religion was excluded from the public sphere. The second led to the establishment of a democratic republic influenced by a mixture of Christian and Enlightenment thinking in which the separation of church and state was crucial, without diminishing the civic role of religion. Thus democracy in France and America had developed differently. American democracy, as Bonhoeffer perceived it, was not founded "on humanitarian principles or human right, but on the kingdom of God and the limitations of earthly powers."[19] If France still struggles today to find the spiritual resources to cement its now religiously plural yet very secular society into a cohesive whole, America has yet to resolve or make more creative the tension between its Enlightenment and Puritan heritages.

Bonhoeffer's observation lays bare, once again, one of the fundamental issues in American politics, namely the role of religion and specifically Christianity in public life. The nation is not only much more religiously plural than previously, but it is polarized along religious lines in ways that it was not when De Tocqueville visited. The divisions are several: between Christians and people of other faith communities, notably Muslims; between religious believers and secularists; and between conservative and fundamentalist Christians on the one hand and liberal-progressive on the other, even if this latter polarity has been largely overcome in

19. Ibid., 451.

the African American churches. Nonetheless, all Americans would agree that religious liberty is essential, most would agree that church and state have to be kept separate, and many insist that faith communities have the right to engage in public life.

But Americans disagree fundamentally on their understanding of the nation. For many white Americans the nation is essentially one of European descent. In addition, for many traditionalists and fundamentalists the United States is a white Anglo-Saxon Christian nation brought into being by God with a theocratic mandate based on the Bible; hence, some ambiguity is evident on the separation of church and state. By contrast, more liberal and progressive Christians accept that America is a secular pluralistic society and insist that human rights are as much based on the teaching of the Hebrew prophets and Jesus as they are on liberal tradition. From these different starting points, Christians in America oppose or support abortion, gay and civil rights, the teaching of evolution in schools, as well as opposition or support for Muslims, Palestinians, or the state of Israel. All of this feeds into the different perceptions of what makes America great or not.

One of Bonhoeffer's teachers at Union Seminary in 1931, and the person responsible for his return in 1939, was Reinhold Niebuhr, the leading public theologian in America at that time. Niebuhr was an influential figure in helping Bonhoeffer understand the social responsibility of Christians and the church. In his book *The Chil-*

dren of Light and the Children of Darkness, published in 1944 at the height of the Second World War, Niebuhr provided a searching critique of the liberal optimism and individualism that characterized American democracy, and insisted that it required a much deeper theological base if it was to become just and equitable. Niebuhr's critique of liberal democracy in America speaks directly to some of the problems facing global democracy today, but more specifically in America, not least its exercise of global power and what Niebuhr called, even back then, "the unpredictable character of American foreign policy."[20]

It is not surprising that political and religious radicalism and fundamentalism flourish in situations of political uncertainty and transition. But a major test of a truly free and democratic society is the extent to which it permits and protects religious freedom—not just the freedom of worship, but also the freedom of prophetic witness. In Niebuhr's words, "One of the greatest problems of democratic civilization is how to integrate the life of its various subordinate, ethnic, religious, and economic groups in the community in such a way that the richness and harmony of the whole community will be enhanced and not destroyed by them."[21]

Some of Niebuhr's deepest insights on democracy

20. Reinhold Niebuhr, *The Children of Light and the Children of Darkness* (New York: Scribner's, 1944), 185.
21. Ibid., 124.

107

are already evident in the Preface to the first edition of his book: "Man's capacity for justice," Niebuhr wrote, "makes democracy possible; but man's inclination to injustice makes democracy necessary."[22] This led him to say that democracy was not primarily about protecting individual rights but controlling the abusive use of power in the interests of justice, especially "if a society should become inclined to impatience with the dangers of freedom."[23] Equally important are Niebuhr's comments on the bourgeois or middle-class character of liberal democracy. In fact, already in 1944, Niebuhr tells us that it "is obvious that democracy, in so far as it is a middle-class ideology, also faces its doom" unless it deepens and broadens its character.[24] In other words, if democracy does not serve the interests of the poor and oppressed it will fail. For a nation to become great, it has to find a way to ensure that there is genuine freedom and meaningful justice for all, and therefore a way for power to be exercised for good not evil. It is also dangerous to assume that the forces pushing toward a democratic world community cannot be stopped or reversed.[25]

No one knew better than Martin Luther King Jr. that democratic theories are not self-fulfilling. For King, democracy in America was fatally flawed both economically and socially because it privileged white cit-

22. Ibid., xiii.
23. Ibid., xiv.
24. Ibid., 3.
25. Ibid., 159.

izens above those of color.[26] A just democracy is an oxymoron in a segregated society; it is only possible in an integrated and pluralistic one. For King, salvation in Christ could be distinguished but also not separated from human rights. There was no unbridgeable gap between the humanitarian vision of democracy and the proclamation of the Hebrew prophets, and no fundamental conflict between Christian witness and political action. In fact, King fused secular and sacred history, and brought them together in a dynamic synthesis of personal salvation and political liberation within the concrete framework of a democracy that was genuinely committed to justice, equality, and freedom.[27]

This blending of prophetic Christianity and the reign of God, along with the more progressive vision of democracy embodied in the American Constitution and Bill of Rights, is one of the most significant contributions King made to the task of revitalizing democracy and making it fully inclusive. At the center was the Civil Rights Movement, which was intended to help America complete the process of democratization that had "taken far too long to develop, but which," as he said in 1961, "is our most powerful weapon for earning world respect and emulation."[28] Only this could make America great in the eyes of the world, great because

26. *A Testament of Hope: The Essential Writings of Martin Luther King, Jr.*, ed. James Melville Washington (San Francisco: Harper & Row, 1986), 314.

27. See Cornel West, *Philosophical Fragments* (Grand Rapids: Eerdmans, 1988), 3–12.

28. "Equality Now: The President Has the Power," in *A Testament of Hope*, 159.

it was morally good. This was important for King, not so that America could boast, but so that it could help in the struggle for human rights everywhere, as it did. King's testimony certainly contributed to the struggle against Apartheid in South Africa.[29] But on the home front, while the passing of the Civil Rights Act was a major step toward creating an inclusive nation based on the Constitution, America has not yet become that nation; it has yet to overcome tribalism in order to become a fully fledged nation.

The deepening and broadening of democracy was King's goal, but the means used to achieve that end was equally critical. In a way that would later be reflected in the legacy of Mandela, King declared: "We must seek democracy and not the substitution of one tyranny for another. Our aim must never be to defeat or humiliate the white man."[30] God, he added, is "interested in the freedom of the whole human race," not just some races or groups or nations. Essential to achieving this end was King's espousal of nonviolent strategies. This lay at the heart of the matter.

The democratic vision that informed the Freedom Charter adopted in 1956 by the African National Congress was the basis for the struggle against Apartheid in South Africa and then became the blueprint for the Constitution of the post-apartheid republic signed into

29. John W. de Gruchy, *Christianity and Democracy: A Theology for a Just World Order* (Cambridge: Cambridge University Press, 1995), 138–39.
30. Martin Luther King Jr., *Stride Towards Freedom: The Montgomery Story* (New York: Harper & Row, 1958), 220.

law by President Nelson Mandela in 1996. Democracy had to become something far more in South Africa than it was in the United States even in King's time. Not only did the South African Constitution insist that the country belongs to "all who live in it," united in diversity, but it also laid "the foundations for a democratic and open society in which government is based on the will of the people and every citizen is equally protected by law."[31]

Despite such advances, many people, not least in Africa, remain skeptical about democracy as a system of government that can truly address the challenges of our time, especially that of poverty. Many of them, after all, live in failed neocolonial states. Their views may be encapsulated in statements such as: "we don't want democracy, we want justice"; "wherever democracy is implemented violence erupts"; "democracy is a Western system of government that is being used to reinforce neocolonialism"; "it is good in theory but not in practice."

There are at least some *prima facie* grounds for all of these objections. So, the seemingly irrevocable democratic impulses that characterized the final decades of the twentieth century are now being viewed with cynicism and skepticism as right-wing nationalisms revive and liberal politics crumble. The sad truth is that democracy does not inevitably result in justice, social

31. Preamble to the Constitution of the Republic of South Africa, November 16, 1996.

stability, and cohesion. Certainly, the postcolonial transition to democracy in sub-Saharan Africa, in Eastern Europe with the collapse of the Soviet Union, in South Arica with the ending of Apartheid, in North Africa and the Middle East following the Arab Spring, and the implosion of Iraq after the American-led invasion, have failed to meet the expectations of so many who were led to believe that democracy was the way ahead. Instead there is rampant corruption and massive changes in technology that have changed the playing fields on which the struggle for democracy is now taking place.

Corruption and "Expertocracy"

Jean Bethke Elshtain published her *Democracy on Trial* in 1995 at the same time that I published my study on *Christianity and Democracy*. She was more pessimistic about the future of democracy than I, maybe because of her location in the United States, a rather "tired democracy," and mine in a South Africa that was flexing its newfound democratic muscle with great enthusiasm. While many then thought that the global expansion of democracy was inevitable following the end of the Cold War and the downfall of Apartheid, for Elshtain its future prospects in established Western democracies was not as bright as assumed and, by extension, failure there could undermine the "new democracies." She wrote about a "culture of mistrust," about "a public whose appetite for scandals" seemed insatiable, and about "declining levels of involvement in politics" that "stokes cynicism about politics and politicians."[32]

This is the situation that we now face as European democratic unity falters, Americanism triumphs, terrorism flourishes, and the majority of the world's population live in poverty. While some applaud Brexit and Trump for simply bringing change by smashing "through the complacent expectations and blinkered preoccupations of a political elite," others are dismayed that "electorates have delivered results that will be self-evidently harmful both to citizens of these nations, and to stability in the wider world." There has, it is said, "been a distinctly authoritarian streak visible, too, from leaders of democracies including India and Turkey. Demagoguery, the scourge of democracy, has reared its head."[33] And the legacy of authoritarian rule, whether Imperial or Communist, prevents democracy from taking firm root in Russia under president Vladimir Putin. The majority of Russians evidently prefer a strong leader who can get things done, to one whose leadership is weakened by too much democracy or the oligarchic corruption that became endemic after the end of the Soviet Union.[34]

In response to the election of Trump and these other developments, Rowan Williams argues that "mass

32. Elshtain, *Democracy on Trial*, 2.

33. *The Guardian*, December 25, 2016.

34. See Archie Brown, *The Myth of the Strong Leader: Political Leadership in the Modern Age* (London: Vintage, 2015), 47ff.

democracy" has failed, and proposes that it is time "to seek a humane alternative." His main point is that "conventional politicians" have failed to understand "the discontent of the disenfranchised and insecure." He also challenges the idea that "there was still a solution available within the politics of a market society, in which ideas are shaped by public demand." The problem lies much deeper, demonstrated by the way in which Trump was able to manipulate the crowds that supported him through "the ersatz politics of mass theatre" in which his aim was to win at all costs, much like the TV shows that made him a household name. As such, says Williams, this is "the most cynical betrayal of those who are disenfranchised," confirming "that they have no part in real political processes; they can only choose their monarch. They have become detached from the work of politics by the erosion of liberties and economic opportunities." Democracy has, in fact,

> been narrowed down to a mechanism for managing large-scale interests in response to explicit and implicit lobbying by fabulously well-resourced commercial and financial concerns. . . . The effect has been a growing assumption that what goes on in public political debate does not represent any voices other than the privileged and self-interested.[35]

35. Rowan Williams, "Mass Democracy Has Failed—It's Time to Seek a Humane Alternative," *New Statesman*, November 17, 2016.

Such democracy does not solve the problems of the poor and powerless, or even the middle-class unemployed. What it does, says Williams, is to deliver "people into the hands of another kind of dishonest politics: the fact-free manipulation of emotion by populist adventurers."

The 2014 decision by the U.S. Supreme Court to strike down aggregate limits on individual contributions to federal candidates and political parties led Thomas Piketty, the French economist, to note that hundreds of millions of U.S. dollars are now given by wealthy supporters to support right-wing political candidates who have become "the symbol of all powerful wealth."[36] He went on to say that

> [t]he share of wealth held by the richest 1 percent in America is approaching the dangerous heights seen in the *Ancien Régime* or *Belle Époque* Europe. For a country founded in large part as an antithesis to Europe's patrimonial societies, it is a rude-awakening.[37]

This "drift to oligarchies" may be most pronounced in America and Russia, but it exists across the world, and South Africa is one of the worst examples, where the gap between the wealthy and the poor is obscenely large. This is exacerbated by the extent to which the rich, throughout Africa as it happens, stash away vast

36. Thomas Piketty, "On Oligarchy in America," in *On Our Troubled Times* (New York: Viking, 2016), 131.
37. Ibid., 132.

sums of their money in overseas tax havens—a fact
that led Piketty to comment that "Africa doesn't need
aid; it simply needs an international legal system that
can prevent it from permanent pillage."[38]

In a hard-hitting critique of neo-liberalism, the
South African economist Sampie Terreblanche refers
to this as part of the "dark side of globalization," in
which large areas of neoliberal capitalist influence are
self-perpetuating and seemingly beyond state control
or that of the United Nations.[39] These not only promote
neocolonial trade to the detriment of the so-called
developing world, but they also support the growth
of the armaments industry and militarism, something
that Trump is massively promoting. Moreover, they
prevent the urgent implementation of environmental
policies that conflict with business interests. As Terreblanche puts it: "The improper intervention of the
corporate sector and the capitalist elite in the process
of political decision-making has undermined the real
purpose of democratic elections quite seriously."[40]
Wealthy oligarchs have tried to capture the resources
of the state for their own purposes. Such corruption
not only leads to the abuse of power that compromises
government integrity and undermines democratic
institutions and process, but it also siphons off huge
amounts of capital from serving the needs of the poor.

38. Piketty, "Capital in South Africa," in *On Our Troubled Times*, 170.
39. Terreblanche, *Western Empires*, 476–83.
40. Ibid., 540.

Unfortunately, the end of such corruption is not in sight.

But there is another dimension to the problem that has now become center stage. This was highlighted in the headline of an article in *The Guardian*, which asked, "Can democracy survive the fourth industrial revolution? Should it?"[41] A subheading put the challenge bluntly: "As automation and digitization undermine employment and increase inequality, established political systems will need to adapt—fast!"

On the one hand, the Internet has opened up a dynamic new possibility for participatory democracy. Potentially, everyone with Internet access can express their opinions and cast their vote in an instant. But, on the other hand, there is a growing hostility among political elites toward any form of real participation of the masses in the processes of government. The feeling is that the vote should only be cast by those who are educated and well informed, otherwise we end up with bad policies and practices that don't serve the interests of the people. From this perspective, only the educated elites can save democracy, what Dallmayr calls an "expertocracy." The problem then becomes that democracy ends up serving their interests and, in effect, becomes rule by the rich for the sake of the rich. This "irretrievably damages social cohesion and democratic beliefs."[42] And when such "expertocracy"

41. Jeff Sparrow, "Can democracy survive the fourth industrial revolution? Should it?" *The Guardian*, January 11, 2017.

is linked to Western cultural and technological developments, it further fuels "charges of neo-colonialism, Eurocentrism, or Western cultural hegemony."[43]

So just when participatory democracy becomes more possible through digital technology, binding people together across the globe to serve their basic needs and work for the common good, there has been "an upsurge in nationalism, xenophobia and overt racism, as well as a growing hostility to global institutions." In addition, levels of political participation in the democratic process seem to have decreased rather than increased, and those organizations that have traditionally enabled participatory democracy to work have become marginalized. The bottom line is clear:

> [T]he primacy of the market in the economic and social developments falling under the rubric of the fourth industrial revolution necessarily predispose elites to what we might call a managerial version of representative democracy—a system in which politicians see their first and foremost responsibility as ensuring voters don't interfere with "sound economic management."[44]

In sum, democracy might still be for the people in some way, but it has little to with their choice and everything to do with who has access to wealth and power.

---

42. Satyajit Das, *A Banquet of Consequences: The Reality of Our Unusually Uncertain Economic Future* (London: Pearson, 2015), 227.
43. Dallmayr, *Dialogue Among Civilizations*, 77.
44. Sparrow, "Can democracy survive?," *The Guardian.*

But dare we simply accept that and resign ourselves to its consequences? Dare we jettison the gains and turn our backs on the promise of democracy? Must we not continue the struggle for a more just and equitable democracy, and so find an alternative democratic future for all?

A More Humane Democracy

At its finest, liberal democracy, drawing on the better side of the European Enlightenment upholds and pursues civil rights and liberties; it is humanist in the best sense of the word. But the blending of liberalism and free-market capitalism in a global environment dominated by Americanism has undermined the social humanism that was fundamental to its early religious roots prior to the Enlightenment and secularization, and is now essential to its survival and recovery.[45]

Ironically, while much of free-market and fundamentalist Americanism claims to be rooted in Calvinist theology and the Protestant work ethic, John Calvin's economic and social thought was far different from the neoliberal capitalist policies and practices that have undermined democracy in the modern world.[46] In fact, his prophetic strictures against the corruption of those in power and those who lived lives of extravagant lux-

45. See de Gruchy, *Christianity and Democracy*, 40–94.
46. André Biéler, *Calvin's Economic and Social Thought* (Geneva: World Council of Churches, 2005).

119

ury while others begged for bread were as frequent and as strident as any social reformer or prophet of any age. And while Calvin firmly cautions against revolutionary uprisings against tyrants, his language suggests that in extreme instances such action might be justified.[47] I stress, fundamentalist American capitalism is a travesty of both the Reformed or Calvinist tradition and Catholic social teaching, but more importantly it is a contradiction of the gospel of Christ. To claim that free-market capitalism is supported by Christianity is not only wrong, but blasphemous.

The only kind of democracy that accords with Christian conviction is a democracy that serves the common good.[48] The same would be affirmed by the best in other faith traditions as it is by advocates of social democracy. For such reasons many committed to democratic renewal today believe that some form of social humanist democracy is vital in dealing with the crisis facing global society. Most fundamentally, the equitable distribution of resources and equal opportunities for all are essential ingredients of a genuinely democratic order. Without this more egalitarian vision and commitment, democracy becomes a means of protecting individual self-interest rather than pursuing the common good and establishing a genuine commonwealth.

47. John Calvin, *Institutes of the Christian Religion*, trans. Ford Lewis Battles, ed. John T. McNeill (Philadelphia: Westminster, 1960 [1536]), IV/xx/31.
48. See de Gruchy, *Christianity and Democracy*, 225–78.

Contemporary struggles for democracy and the debates they have evoked, particularly with regard to gender, cultural identity, sexuality, and economic issues, have therefore made it necessary to go beyond the rather sterile debate between liberalism and socialism. In Williams' words,

> The conventional accounts of what is "right" and "left" are fast becoming tribal signals, rather than useful moral categories. The leviathans of the party system will sooner or later have to look at their structures and accountability—not as a step to plebiscite populism, but in terms of what they can do to nurture discussion and decision in the actual communities to which people (not The People) belong.[49]

The struggle for a new global democratic order is therefore not a matter of extending liberal Western democracy to places where this does not exist; but of developing a genuinely humane democratic order in different contexts that is able to protect and further human rights, and promote the common good. This is equally necessary in countries that have a long tradition of democracy, but where the struggle for a just democracy has, as it were, come to a standstill. For democracy to flourish today it has to be crafted in such a way that it serves the cause of justice, equality, and freedom, rather than remain trapped in past expres-

49. Rowan Williams, "Mass Democracy Has Failed," *New Statesman*, November 17, 2016.

sions of democracy that serve the self-interest of entrenched elites alone. This requires the reawakening and strengthening of the organs of civil society without which a nation cannot achieve greatness. But this cannot happen without the training of leaders and the emergence of prophets who can inspire the next generation and take us into the future. This is a challenge to the churches and other faith communities, for it has often been from within them that such leaders and prophets have arisen.

4

Who Are the Leaders We Need?

The prophets prophesy falsely,
and the priests rule as the prophets direct;
my people love to have it so,
but what will you do when the end comes?
                                    —Jeremiah the prophet[1]

. . . [I]n a time of pestilence there are more things to
admire in men than to despise. None the less, Dr Rieux
knew that the tale he had to tell could not be one of final
victory. It could only be the record of what had to be
done, and what assuredly would have to be done again

1. Jer 31:31.

> in the never-ending fight against terror and its relent-
> less onslaughts, despite their personal afflictions, by all
> who, while unable to be saints but refusing to bow down
> to pestilence, strive their utmost to be healers.
>
> —Albert Camus[2]

The year is 2073. A Dark Age has fallen on Western
civilization. You go onto the cosmic internet to find
the reasons, and discover a long-forgotten report on
"The Collapse of Western Civilization." What you read
is half-expected, but still shocking. Self-deception, a
denial of scientific predictions, and an ideological fixa-
tion on "free" markets "disabled the world's powerful
nations" and "led to the Great Collapse and Mass
Migration."[3] On checking the sources, you are led to
believe that the author is a Chinese historian who
based his conclusions on research done in our own
time. But you later discover that the Report was written by two contemporary American social scientists
who, on the basis of their research, concluded that we
are living in the end times of our civilization.

It is now 2017 not 2073, so we can read for ourselves
their startling conclusion that despite having all the
information we have at our disposal to avoid catastrophe, we deny reality, deceive ourselves, and so are

2. Albert Camus, *The Plague*, trans. Stuart Gilbert (London: Penguin, 1966),
251–52.
3. Naomi Oreskes and Erik M. Conway, "The Collapse of Western Civilization:
A View from the Future," in *Daedalus, the Journal of the American Academy of
Arts & Sciences* 142, no. 1 (Winter 2013): 41.

impotent to prevent the inevitable. We hear what is said but do not listen, we read what is written but do not take it to heart, and so fail to act responsibly for the sake of future generations. In the haunting words of Naomi Oreskes and Erik Conway, who wrote the report:

> While analysts differ on the details, virtually all agree that the people of Western civilization knew what was happening to them but were unable to stop it. Indeed, the most startling aspect of the story is just how much these people knew, yet how little they acted upon what they knew.[4]

We have more reports, analyses, information, and resolutions than we can process, let alone implement. We know what to do, but it seems we lack the political, moral, and spiritual will to act timeously and decisively. In talking about the "end times," Jesus made the same point with reference to the ancient story of Noah. People do not take Noah's weather report seriously, they just go on "eating and drinking, marrying and being given in marriage."[5] We only wake up when the floods come and the earthquakes strike, when terror rudely disturbs the comfortable tenor of our lives, when economies collapse and the Four Horsemen of the Apocalypse wreak havoc yet again.

Given the endless debates on the critical issues facing us at countless regional and international confer-

4. Oreskes and Conway, "The Collapse of Western Civilization," 40–41.
5. Luke 17:22–37.

ences, and the watered-down resolutions adopted, there is reason to blame this failure to take timely and decisive action on the lack of good leadership. But this begs some important questions, especially in democratic societies. After all, we citizens elect our leaders and support them. We are all in this together, and while some are doing their utmost to prevent disaster, many more of us are apathetic bystanders. The least we could do is to hold our leaders to account.

This is what transpired in the presidential election in America, the Brexit vote, and the elections that followed across Europe. People had had enough of a leadership that, so it seemed to them, had miserably failed. They might not have understood all the issues, or even cared to understand them, they might even have voted in ways that were not actually to their benefit, but they wanted leaders who could bring about change. The no vote over Brexit, and the yes vote for Trump, were not simply votes against being part of Europe or votes for the Republican Party, but votes against leaders they believed were out of touch with the reality they experienced daily. They were no longer prepared to leave their own and their children's destiny in the hands of a political elite they no longer trusted. They wanted a place in Noah's Ark not just in order to survive, but also to flourish, even if it meant keeping others out of the Ark for lack of space and resources. But that, of course, is the problem.

People and nations are beginning to wake up, to

flex their collective political muscle, but too often they are motivated by self-interest rather than the common good of all, whether within their countries or further afield. That is why the dissemination of scientific research is essential, why we need a free and responsible press and informed citizens, and why we need to be producing more and better leaders. Nations and global society as a whole cannot be just and humane without good leadership, and that requires informed and active civil societies and faith communities.

On receiving the 2016 *Die Welt* Literature Prize in Berlin, the British novelist Zadie Smith likened us all to "complex musical scores from which certain melodies can be teased out and others ignored or suppressed, depending, at least in part, on who is doing the conducting." She continued: "At this moment, all over the world—and most recently in America—the conductors standing in front of this human orchestra have only the meanest and most banal melodies in mind." But, she reminded her German audience, that those "martial songs" that whipped up support for Hitler are no longer "a very distant memory." In fact, wrote Smith, "there is no place on earth where they have not been played at one time or another," and exhorted those who remember "a finer music" to now "play it, and encourage others, if we can, to sing along."[6]

6. Zadie Smith, "On Optimism and Despair," *The New York Review of Books*, December 22, 2016.

The Next Generation

While it is striking that so many people who have previously been apathetic about politics are now more politically engaged, it is equally striking that this is true of many of the younger generation, the "millennials," who have come of political age and lost confidence in the leadership of their elders. In the United States some of them voted for Trump, and many for Bernie Sanders's more egalitarian vision. It is too early to tell whether this is simply an expression of the perennial cyclic conflict between generations, or a political awakening that has more lasting consequences. But however this may be, what has been observed is that the more general anger and frustration of young people is greater in countries where there is a large or growing population of educated young people. It is also the case that a quarter of the world's population is now between the ages of fifteen and thirty, and that many of them, if educated and skilled, are unemployed, and many others are unemployable.[7] They are disillusioned, resentful, and some are not just willing to protest but even to change the world by violence.

This is also the digital generation that is in command of technologies that enable them instantly to share hopes, fears, ideas, information, plans, and tactics.

7. Pankaj Mishra, *Age of Anger: A History of the Present* (London: Allen Lane, 2017), 330–31.

And, as Pankaj Mishra observes, this "has altered individual and collective ways of being in the world."[8] There is, he writes, "much more longing than can be realized legitimately in the age of freedom and entrepreneurship; more desires for objects of consumption than can be fulfilled by actual income; more dreams than can be fused with stable society by redistribution and greater opportunity." In addition, there are more discontented people whose demands can be satisfied by politics, traditional therapies, or legal means and more stimulus "than can be converted into action."[9]

But this is not primarily a generational issue. Thoughtful young people do not invariably reject the wisdom of their elders. But they are likely to reject the opinions and actions of leaders, irrespective of age, who lack integrity, moral courage, wisdom, and the ability to listen to their fears and hopes. They are looking for authentic voices who can articulate their discontent in a way that makes sense, relates to their experience, and can offer a way forward. That is the voice of the true leader as well as the true prophet.

Bonhoeffer had a keen interest in the next generation. In May 1944 he prepared a sermon in prison for the baptism of his godson, Dietrich Bethge. In it he confesses that his own generation, which had allowed Hitler to seize power, had "learned too late that it is not the thought but readiness to take responsibility

8. Ibid., 334–35.
9. Ibid., 340–41.

that is the mainspring of action." He went on to express the hope that the next generation would not fail in the same way.[10] Shortly after, in a letter to his nephew, Hans-Walter Schleicher, he asked him what his generation thought were "the guideposts of their lives."[11] He then commented: "After all, the most important question for the future is how we are going to find a basis for living together with other people, what spiritual realities and rules we honour as the foundations for a meaningful human life."

Bonhoeffer's question remains one of the most urgent facing us today. Our struggle for a more just, compassionate, and sustainable world is a struggle about those values that bind together all generations who are concerned about the future. Or in Bonhoeffer's own words: "The ultimately responsible question is not how I extricate myself heroically from a situation but how a coming generation is to go on living. Only from such a historically responsible question will fruitful solutions arise."[12] Bonhoeffer returns to the theme in a further passage:

> There are people who think it frivolous and Christians who think it is impious to hope for a better future on earth and to prepare for it. They believe in chaos, disorder, and catastrophe, perceiving it in what is happening now. They withdraw in resignation or pious flight from

10. Bonhoeffer, *Letters and Papers from Prison*, 387.
11. Ibid., 409.
12. Bonhoeffer, "After ten years," *Letters and Papers from Prison*, 42.

the world, from responsibility for ongoing life, for build-ing anew, for the coming generations.[13]

Most informed citizens, old and young alike, and irre-spective of locality, know that we have to find a way to overcome the gap between rich and poor; we know that short-term self-interest leads to halfhearted mea-sures to address the problem; we know that working for peace is an imperative that demands our best efforts, but we continue to build weapons of mass destruction that bleed our economies and soon become obsolete; we know about the escalating dangers facing the environment in which we live and the measures we can take to prevent ecological disaster, but we are tardy in doing so. We may even know that the failure to act now on what we know is more dangerous and has more serious consequences because we face "the end" more than ever before, even if it is not yet. Larry Ras-mussen puts his finger on the problem:

> . . . Planet Home is undergoing a transformational moment, akin to those "ages" that come to pass as episodes in geologic time. But this one is different, at least for us, since it is happening not only in geologic time but in human time as well. Moreover, the brainy species is not only around for this episode but is among its causes, its reason for geophysical change.[14]

13. Bonhoeffer, *Letters and Papers from Prison*, 51.
14. Larry L. Rasmussen, *Earth-Honoring Faith: Religious Ethics in a New Key* (New York: Oxford University Press, 2013), 4.

131

This is the timeframe within which the rest of our woes are set. And it is within this framework that we have to ask what kind of people we should become, and what kind of leaders we need—and definitely don't need.

True and False Leaders

In his teaching about the "end times," Jesus warned that there would be false messiahs ready to respond to the roars of adoring crowds and ready to fill any leadership vacuum. These misleaders, he said, were "thieves and robbers" or "wolves in sheep's clothing." Such power-hungry authoritarian leaders arise in times of crisis because there is a failure of good leadership and a clamor for strong leadership. Christians should never forget that the choice Pilate, a Roman consul, gave the people of Jerusalem, was between Barabbas, a revolutionary zealot who would resort to violence in fighting the imperialists, and Jesus, whose chosen path was victory for humanity via the cross. The clamor of the people, who certainly had good reason to revolt against Rome and their own Temple authorities, was for a strong leader, not a prophet who proclaimed justice for the alien, love for the enemy, and forgiveness for the guilty.

Hitler could not have come to power in 1933 without the support of a large number of ordinary Germans who felt they had legitimate grievances he alone could satisfy. Populist leaders have no future without people who feel they have no future, people without genuine or perceived grievances. He also could not have come to power unless there were high-ranking generals, industrialists, politicians, and even world leaders, who gave him their support despite reservations, believing that they could keep him under control and even use him for their own ends. But despots and demagogues are not normally fools, and it is our folly to underestimate their ability and political cunning in serving their own interests, and that of their kith, kin, and ilk. They know how to manipulate the masses by appealing to their basest instincts: fear, hatred, racism. They know what to promise them in times of uncertainty and crisis: work, security, a sense of identity and purpose, the fulfillment of their dreams. And they know how to seize the moment. They also know how to debunk their critics, ignore scientific reports, silence the media, and propagate half-truths that morph into lies. They know how to make sure their followers believe in them, so that what they say is true even if it is false.

From the outset, there were many people who might have been expected to recognize the danger that Hitler presented, but failed to do so because of their own interests. After all, his promises also resonated with the hopes of many, and his rhetoric touched the core of their nationalist and patriotic emotions. They were therefore prepared to trust him as their Leader. But there were also those who recognized Hitler for what he was, and were determined to oppose him. The Bonhoeffer family was among them. But Hitler's opponents soon discovered that reason, decency, morality, and truth could not withstand brutal power, propaganda, and the tidal wave of popular emotion, without an immense struggle. If they were not imprisoned they were silenced. But perhaps they also failed, as Bonhoeffer said in his letter to his nephew, because they did not put thought into action soon enough. Once the communists and other vocal political opponents had been disposed of, there were few standing firm enough to put a spoke in the wheel of a juggernaut out of control.

Early in 1933, the German broadcasting authority, which was not yet fully under Nazi control, invited various theologians and academics to speak on radio about the issues facing the "younger generation." Bonhoeffer was the second in line, and his talk, broadcast from Berlin on February 1st, was given just two days after Hitler was enthusiastically acclaimed Chancellor of the Third Reich.

He began by identifying three groups of disenchanted young people, not unlike many today. Those who had fought in the First World War (or we might say, veterans of Vietnam, the struggle against Apartheid, the war in Iraq); the next generation, those who were too young to have fought in the War but had lived through the calamities that followed: economic uncertainty, unemployment, inadequate healthcare and social services. And now there was a new generation that had, said Bonhoeffer, "reached maturity during a period of history during which the previously well-established Western world came apart at the seams." Bonhoeffer straddled these generations, and he knew each generation well. He knew that the new generation was trying desperately to find a foothold and a leader who would not let them down as their elders had been misled, someone who could truly lead them into the future. But what kind of leader, or Führer, could do this?

Given the failures of the Weimar government and its eventual collapse, Bonhoeffer not only feared the rise of authoritarian demagogues, he also did not have much confidence in the popular democratic process to choose the leaders that Germany now needed. A strong leader was required, but one who could exercise the necessary authority and power without abusing it. His discussion of the issues is complex. But critical was the distinction he made between the individual as leader, and the office of leadership. A strong charismatic individual who embodies the populist hopes of the masses by projecting a divine aura may have authority "from below" as it were, but is usually a false leader. By contrast, true leaders derive their authority, not from their personality, but from their office. They function within constitutional limits according to the rule of law; that is, for Bonhoeffer, their office is "from above."[15] Leaders chosen by popular vote are not thereby God's choice; only leaders who respect their office, for that is God's gift.

By analogy Bonhoeffer speaks of the leader as a "father-figure" who replaces the one who went to war and did not return, the father who is absent or has failed to exercise his proper role in the family. There is, Bonhoeffer said, "a decisive difference between the authority of the father, the teacher, the judge, the statesman, on the one hand, and the authority of the leader, on the other."[16] Such a *Führer*, who comes to power through the will of the masses because of the failure of social structures and responsibilities, is "an idol the led are looking for,"[17] but he is nothing other than a *Verführer* (misleader) whose misappropriation of power will eventually crush him.[18]

There can be little doubt that those who listened to Bonhoeffer's radio address knew who he was talking about, which is probably the reason why the broadcasting authorities cut him off before he completed his talk. But while he had made it clear that a true and good leader respected the rule of law, he had not said what made such a leader great in a time of crisis and impending doom.

15. Bonhoeffer, *Berlin 1933*, Dietrich Bonhoeffer Works, vol. 12, ed. Larry Rasmussen (Minneapolis: Fortress Press, 2009), 278.
16. Ibid., 279.
17. Ibid., 280.
18. Ibid., 281.

What Makes a Leader Great?

The skills required of a pope or an archbishop are not identical with the skills required of a president or premier, the CEO of a business corporation, or those of a priest, social prophet, university professor, police officer, member of parliament, or manager of a store. Each office has its own requisite skills. Likewise there are variables that need to be kept in mind, for leadership is always contextual. What may be possible and appropriate in one context is not necessarily so in another. War, for example, may require a certain kind of leader who, in another context, namely a stable and peaceful democracy, would make him or her unsuitable.[19] Even so, there is a common core of leadership skills that characterize great leaders, and the more the authority the more such skills are needed even if possessing them all is beyond the capacity of most. It is this core that needs to be identified and strengthened at every level according to the gifts and abilities of the demands of the particular office and the context in which a leader serves.

This common core is as more about character than the nuts and bolts of running a church, university, business empire, or country. That is why leadership training is not just about equipping people with technical skills, but shaping and forming their characters

19. Archie Brown, *The Myth of the Strong Leader: Political Leadership in the Modern Age* (London: Vintage, 2015), 24–61.

so that they can recognize and exercise the skills needed, and be open and willing to appropriate them. Some of these may come naturally to some leaders, but they also need to be discerned, enabled, and developed. Leadership formation is about ensuring that those called to lead are able to do so. To decry the lack of good leaders without taking steps to produce them is folly and could be fatal; it is as foolish as knowing what to do but failing to do what is needed to avoid disaster.

In his timely book, *The Myth of the Strong Leader*, written shortly before the presidential race that brought Trump to the White House, the distinguished political scientist Archie Brown questions the view that only what we commonly call "strong leaders" can solve our problems and lead us safely through the troubled waters of the crises we face. In order to provide a profile of a good or great leader, by contrast to that of the mythical "strong leader," Brown takes us on a tour de force of political leadership ranging from autocratic to democratic through the ages, across continents, cultures, and diverse contexts. The key words he uses to describe a great leader are, on reflection, self-evident: integrity, intelligence, discernment, collegiality, vision, critical thinking; being open to considering alternative views; ability to grasp information and express ideas clearly; courage, empathy, and energy.

Few leaders embody all these virtues and skills, but good leaders who become great leaders strive to do so. That is why they build strong moral communities concerned about the common good irrespective of the sphere in which they work. This is critical both for understanding the creation and sustenance of civil society and faith communities such as churches. Good and great leaders encourage the very same qualities that define their leadership, among those they lead. Demagogues produce puppets. Good and great leaders help form communities of people that have integrity, are able to express their views clearly, who listen to and respect each other, are critical yet caring, imaginative and open, courageous and visionary. It is from such communities that prophets of justice and compassion arise because such communities are themselves just and caring.

Apart from debunking the popular idea of a strong leader and reminding us that charismatic leaders are not, as such, good or bad, Brown makes an important distinction within the category of "good leadership," that is, between leadership that is "redefining" and that which is "transformative." Redefining leaders stretch the boundaries of what is regarded as possible and, in so doing, alter the political agenda.[20] Transformational leaders go further, taking reform to a new level. They make a decisive contribution to the economic or political system. Such leaders are rare in democratic societies, but they are not revolutionaries who overthrow the system and institute a more auto-

20. Ibid., 5; see also 101–47.

cratic, often totalitarian form of government. Transformational leaders are democrats who enlarge and
deepen democracy.[21]

Much of the crisis we now face has to do with the
paucity of good leadership in these apocalyptic times,
a leadership that does not capitulate to "populism" but
is able to deepen democracy where it is relatively long
established, or enable the transition from authoritarian to democratic rule where that is being pursued. If
this is so, then the commitment of leaders to democratic values is critical. "Leaders," writes Brown, "who
believe they have a personal right to dominate decision-making in many different areas of policy, and who
attempt to exercise such a prerogative, do a disservice
both to good governance and to democracy. They
deserve not followers, but critics."[22] They may be
charismatic leaders, but they have no respect for their
office that gives them genuine authority.

There is a great deal about the qualities of leadership
in the teaching of Jesus, not least when he is speaking
about the "end times." In such times, Jesus said, people
look for a shepherd to lead them to greener pastures,
one who will give his life for his sheep if necessary
in order that they may have life to the full.[23] This has
often been spiritually romanticized, but in fact Jesus
was speaking directly into the political crisis of his day,

21. Ibid., 6–7; see also 148–93.
22. Ibid., 362.
23. John 10:1–10.

something his hearers would have immediately recognized. The "shepherds of Israel" in the Hebrew Bible refer to Israel's kings. It was an appropriate metaphor because King David had been a shepherd, and he knew the difference between a good one and a bad.[24] So David understood God's authority and character in the same terms.[25] He knew he was called to rule as God's representative in the same way.

But too often the "shepherds of Israel," including David, failed in their responsibilities, as the prophets repeatedly declared.[26] Hence the hope for a leader, one anointed by God (i.e., a messiah) who would come to "redeem Israel" and liberate her from oppression. Jesus referred to this as "servant leadership," and he held it out as an example for his disciples:

> You know that the rulers of the Gentiles lord it over them, and their great ones are tyrants over them. It will not be so among you; but whoever wishes to be great among you must be your servant . . . just as the Son of Man came not to be served but to serve, and to give his life for many.[27]

To argue that political leaders have to lead differently than other leaders, say religious ones, is to miss the point Jesus is making. He is speaking precisely about

24. See 2 Sam 7:7–8.
25. Psalm 23.
26. Ezek 34:1–10.
27. Matt 20:25–28.

141

those who should lead Israel, not spiritual gurus but political rulers. It is not just idealistic and romantic to expect that political leaders, especially those who claim to be Christian, should heed Jesus's words and follow his example in being servants of the people they lead. And there *are* models of such political leaders who understood what Jesus was saying and whose example we need to recall. One of them was Chief Albert Luthuli.

In November 1952 the Apartheid government dismissed Luthuli from his position as a chief in Zululand because of his opposition to apartheid.[28] He later became the first South African winner of the Nobel Peace Prize, on which occasion he gave a speech titled "The Road to Freedom is via the Cross." In it, he explained why he had decided to continue the struggle for freedom and democracy even at the expense of losing his chieftainship. "It is inevitable," he said, "that in working for Freedom some individuals and some families must take the lead and suffer. The Road to Freedom," he continued, "is via the CROSS."[29] Luthuli was banished to Groutville, a small rural town, where he died in 1965, murdered, some say, by agents of Apartheid. But as he said in his speech, "a chief is primarily a servant of his people. He is the voice of his

---

28. See Albert Luthuli, *Let My People Go* (London: Collins, 1962), 125–32.
29. Albert Luthuli, "The Road to Freedom Is Via the Cross," in *Luthuli: Speeches of Albert John Luthuli, 1898–1967*, ed. E.S. Reddy (Durban: Madiba Publishers, 1991), 42.

people."[30] Such leaders are willing to give their lives for their people.

The same was true of Nelson Mandela. By virtue of his position in his clan, Mandela was born to lead, but his skills, inherent as many of them were, were developed as he observed in his youth how Chief Jonginthaba Dalindyebo of the Thembu tribe would conduct affairs at the tribal Great Place. There he learned the fundamental principles of leadership. "I have always endeavored to listen to what each and every person in a discussion had to say before venturing my own opinion," he later wrote.[31] These skills were then honed through his Methodist missionary education, his exposure to political thought at the University of Fort Hare, and his twenty-seven years of imprisonment. All of this prepared him for his leadership role in the struggle against Apartheid and eventually in making the fateful decision to embark on the armed struggle.

Since its founding in 1912, the ANC was committed to nonviolent resistance to colonialism and apartheid for two main reasons. The first was strategic. Born out of the ashes of repeated bloody attempts to repulse colonialism by military means, it was inconceivable that white domination could be challenged by a further recourse to arms. The second was moral. Its ethos

30. Ibid., 40.
31. Nelson Mandela, *Long Walk to Freedom* (Johannesburg: Macdonald Purnell, 1995), 25. See also Brown, *The Myth of the Strong Leader*, 183–89.

was deeply influenced by Christian and democratic values, which were fundamental to the way in which Mandela understood his role as a leader. He was not just a charismatic leader, but one who exercised his leadership within and on behalf of a community of those committed to justice. But he was also a leader who, like Bonhoeffer, as we shall see, dared to take the risk of "free responsibility" in extreme morally ambiguous situations.[32] This was at the heart of the dilemma facing the ANC when, on December 16, 1961, under the leadership of Mandela, it embarked on the armed struggle. The step was taken very reluctantly and against Luthuli's wishes. But as Mandela later stated from the stand during his trial for treason he could do no other if he was to stand firm and lead his people.

> It was only when all else failed, when all channels of peaceful protest were barred to us, that the decision was taken to embark on violent forms of political struggle. . . . We did so not because we desired such a course, but solely because the government had left us with no other choice.[33]

Later, when reflecting back on the role of a leader, after some disagreement with his colleagues just

32. John W. de Gruchy, "Dietrich Bonhoeffer, Nelson Mandela and the Dilemma of Violent Resistance in Retrospect," *Stellenbosch Theological Journal*, 2 no. 1 (2016): 43–60.
33. Nelson Mandela, "Second Court Statement, 1964," in *The Struggle Is My Life* (New York: Pathfinder, 1990) 168.

before the ANC came to power in 1994, Mandela wrote that a leader had to first create a vision, then a following who would help to implement the vision, and then to manage the process through carefully selected teams.[34] If his ability to listen and seek both strategic and moral consensus describes Mandela's secret of success as a democratic leader rather than a revolutionary grasping for power, this describes well how that leadership could be meshed with his role as a revolutionary leader who brought about democratic transformation.

Leaders such as Luthuli and Mandela, even if they do not always agree, have such integrity, courage, vision, and commitment to justice in the service of peace that they not only lead, they also inspire those who follow them to live and act in the same way. In standing firm themselves, they enable others to stand firm with them.

Prophets as True Patriots

There is another form of leadership, one not discussed by Archie Brown in *The Myth of the Strong Leader*, which is always necessary but especially critical in apocalyptic times, namely that of prophet. This is not to speak of prophets who predict the "end times" or assume political office, but those prophets who speak truth to power and do so as part of their patriotic duty.

There are many contemporary models of such

---

34. Nelson Mandela, *Conversations with Myself* (London: Macmillan, 2010), 413.

prophetic leadership. They are not confined to the Christian tradition, and many would identify themselves as secular humanists. But among Christians, some names immediately trip off the tongue: Dag Hammarskjöld, the global peace-maker as first Secretary General of the United Nations, Thomas Merton, Dorothy Day, and Martin Luther King Jr., among Americans; Cardinal Oscar Romero and Pope Francis, among Latin Americans; and Beyers Naudé, Steve Biko, Desmond Tutu, and Allan Boesak, among South Africans. There are many others, women and men, of all nationalities, some well known and some not, who could be added to this list.

All of them are different from each other, but they are united in their faith, courage, hope, compassion, sense of justice, and ability to speak the truth to power, and all of them are examples of true patriotism. Each has also drawn deeply from the wells of Christian spirituality and some from the insights of other traditions. Each in turn has inspired all of us who seek to be faithful in our commitment to Christ, and therefore to justice and peace. And, significantly, each was nurtured in and sustained by a community that has enabled them to become prophets. Prophets might end up feeling very lonely, just as they will almost inevitably suffer for their convictions, but they are surrounded and sustained by many who, as Elijah was reminded, "have not bowed the knee to Baal." Bonhoeffer was such a prophet.

Oddly, some of those who have turned to Bonhoeffer in recent years for inspiration are fundamentalists who supported and voted for Trump. In doing so many have been influenced by the Bonhoeffer biography written by Eric Metaxas.[35] But how does Metaxas, a well-known right-wing American television and radio personality who supports Trump, understand Bonhoeffer? He certainly praises his courageous opposition to Nazism, but fails to relate Bonhoeffer's critique to the resurgence of right-wing nationalism today, and instead aims his criticism at liberal Protestants. In short, Metaxas domesticates Bonhoeffer in support of his neoconservative and fundamentalist Americanism.[36]

To be fair, it must be said that sometimes more liberal Bonhoeffer devotees have erred in their misappropriation of Bonhoeffer's legacy in supporting their agendas. But no Bonhoeffer scholar of any merit would ever consider him giving legitimacy to Americanism. In fact, Bonhoeffer's close friend Bethge, who shared his convictions, likened the Americanism he experienced at Lynchburg College in Virginia, the intellectual home of fundamentalism, to the German Christianity that had supported Nazism.[37] Indeed, in a letter to his

35. Eric Metaxas, *Bonhoeffer: Pastor, Martyr, Prophet, Spy* (Nashville: Nelson, 2010).
36. See Stephen R. Haynes, *The Bonhoeffer Phenomenon* (Minneapolis: Fortress Press, 2004).
37. See Eberhard Bethge, Preface to Keith W. Clements, *A Patriotism for Today: Love of Country in Dialogue with the Witness of Dietrich Bonhoeffer* (London: Collins, 1986), vi–vii.

grandmother in August 1933, in which he bemoans the capitulation of the church to Hitler, Bonhoeffer adds: "The issue is really Germanism or Christianity, and the sooner the conflict comes out into the open, the better."[38]

Bonhoeffer, who was deeply influenced by the great Hebrew prophets, felt a special affinity with Jeremiah who attacked the false court prophets of his day much as Bonhoeffer opposed the German Christian leadership in his day. Later, in prison, Bonhoeffer wrote a sermon for the baptism of his godson Dietrich Bethge in which he said that one day the time would come when prophets would again speak the Word of God "in such a way that the world is changed and renewed." It will be proclaimed, he said, "in a new language . . . the language of a new righteousness and truth, a language proclaiming that God makes peace with humankind and that God's kingdom is drawing near."[39] This is true prophecy. It is not predicting the end times, but speaking the prophetic Word in these penultimate times.

Much of Bonhoeffer's theological reflections in prison, which Metaxas brushes aside, had to do with the recovery of this liberating and redeeming language of justice, truth, and peace, in a "world come of age." This was no academic matter but a call for a radical change in the life of the church and of Christians in

38. To Julie Bonhoeffer, August 20, 1933, in Bonhoeffer, *Berlin 1933*, 150.
39. "Thoughts on the Day of Baptism of Dietrich Bethge," May 1944, Bonhoeffer, *Letters and Papers from Prison*, 437.

order to stand with Jesus in solidarity with the oppressed.[40] Like John the Baptist, Bonhoeffer was preparing the way for a radical understanding of Christian proclamation that goes beyond the Law and the commandment in the light of the gospel and transforms the world.[41]

The global situation that confronts us today is admittedly complex and as such defies simplistic analysis. But prophetic theologians, in the mold of Bonhoeffer, have to take risks in identifying the present moment as a *kairos* that demands a prophetic response. And Bonhoeffer's greatest risk in the interests of justice and peace had yet to be taken.

On June 14, 1940, Paris surrendered to Germany without a fight. Denmark and Norway were already occupied, and Italy had joined forces with Germany. Hitler's popularity at home was at an all-time high. Earlier, in March, the Confessing Church seminary at Finkenwalde was shut down by the Gestapo, and Bonhoeffer, its director, returned to Berlin. The Nazis seemed invincible. Yet, in the shadowy underground, resistance movements were beginning to form. One, made up of high-ranking military officers in the Military Intelligence or *Abwehr*, a sworn enemy of the Gestapo, included Hans von Dohnanyi, Bonhoeffer's brother-in-law and a government lawyer. Von

40. See Bonhoeffer, *Letters and Papers from Prison*, 26–27.
41. See Bonhoeffer, *The Young Bonhoeffer: 1918-1927*, Dietrich Bonhoeffer Works, vol. 9, ed. Hans Pfeifer (Minneapolis: Fortress Press, 2002), 348–49.

Dohnanyi invited Dietrich to join the group in plotting the assassination of Hitler. Bonhoeffer agreed and was drafted into the *Abwehr* to give him military exemption and freedom to travel.

Bonhoeffer's primary task was to develop contacts outside Germany with significant persons in Allied countries with whom he had already some relationship. He was also involved in helping Jews flee from Germany into Switzerland. But he had the further task of helping his co-conspirators deal with a major moral dilemma. Having made a solemn oath to obey Hitler and defend Germany, they were now plotting the Führer's death and their nation's defeat. These men of high moral principle and patriotism were secular humanists who had lost all respect for the church because it had failed so abysmally to oppose Hitler. Like Albert Camus's Dr. Rieux, they were "unable to be saints" but refused "to bow down to pestilence," and so strived "their utmost to be healers." Making common cause with them was, for Bonhoeffer, not a betrayal but a consequence of his faith and part of his pastoral responsibility. But what they were planning was high treason and murder, however dressed up, so they turned to Bonhoeffer for counsel. And as a pastor who lived by the Sermon on the Mount, Bonhoeffer also had to deal with his own conscience.

By now Bonhoeffer was well aware of what was happening in the death camps, and of many other Nazi policies and practices that raised serious ethical questions. He was also sadly aware of the failure of the church to stand firm against Nazism and felt closer to secular humanists like his co-conspirators than he did to the many Christians and church leaders who had remained silent when they should have spoken. So in between his travels on behalf of the Resistance, and in moments of retreat at the Benedictine monastery in Ettal in Bavaria, Bonhoeffer began work on his *Ethics.* And in seeking to justify his involvement in the Resistance and the plot on Hitler's life, Bonhoeffer wrote about the "ethics of free responsibility" that was guiding his actions.[42]

There come moments when Christians have to risk acting in ways that in normal circumstances might be regarded as sinful. Participation in the plot against Hitler was such an exceptional moment, a "*kairos* moment" in which evil was being called good, and true patriotism was condemned as treason. To stand aloof from what needed to be done at such a time was worse than getting his hands dirty in assisting in the assassination of Hitler and helping to bring his country to its knees. For Bonhoeffer, genuine patriotism demanded that he engage in treason, for that was what love of country now required. Bonhoeffer loved Germany so much, that he both prayed and worked for its defeat.[43]

The unqualified devotion of citizens to their country

---

42. Bonhoeffer, *Ethics,* 79–81.
43. See Eberhard Bethge, *Dietrich Bonhoeffer: A Biography*, ed. Victoria J. Barnett (Minneapolis: Fortress Press, 2000), 675.

has always been the basis of a nation's power. This is the essence of patriotism that leads to acts of great unselfishness on behalf of one's country, especially in times of war. It is, as Reinhold Niebuhr wrote in 1932 as nationalism was becoming rampant, "a high form of altruism" that "expresses itself, on occasion, with such fervor that the critical attitude of the individual toward the nation . . . is almost completely destroyed."[44] Right-wing nationalist dictators and demagogues and their followers always depend on such uncritical allegiance from their followers and try to coerce the citizenry as a whole to fall into line. They can brook no criticism whether from the press or the pulpit, or from pacifists who refuse to fight their wars.

From the beginning of Christianity, the followers of Jesus have always been uneasy about such unconditional support for country, king, or president, something that compromised their loyalty to Jesus as Lord. This is precisely why Caesar threw them to the lions, and why it was a great relief when Christendom gave Christianity a legal status. But this status came with a price. To obey Jesus as Lord required obeying the emperor unconditionally as well. Even the words of Jesus, "Give to Caesar the things that are Caesar's," were now used, as they still are, to justify this dual allegiance, without pausing for a moment to consider the fact that this could not include ultimate, only penulti-

44. Reinhold Niebuhr, *Moral Man and Immoral Society* (New York: Scribner's, 1960), 91.

mate, loyalty. Patriotism had to be qualified by obedience to Christ.

Keith Clements, who has best examined the development of Bonhoeffer's critical patriotism, and applied it especially to Christian witness in Britain, puts it clearly when he writes that a Christian perspective "will strongly qualify the ideal of national loyalty today."[45] This, Clements says, does not mean abolishing patriotism as a virtue, but recognizing its provisional or penultimate status. The nation does, of course, deserve and require the loyalty of its citizens, but only when acting for the common good, and that implies not only the good of one's country but of the world as a whole. Such loyalty must take the form of criticism when the nation begins to act badly in its own selfish interests, and this, as in the case of Bonhoeffer, might require not just protest but resistance. The Christian can never love his or her country truly without this reservation.

In the struggle against Apartheid and in the transition to democracy, South Africa was blessed by many true patriots, two of whom stand as exemplars. One of them was the Afrikaner Dutch Reformed minister, Beyers Naudé, the other one Nelson Mandela. Naudé, like Bonhoeffer, came from the upper crust of his people and was destined to lead South Africa as a devoted nationalist. But his Christian faith and love for both his own people and for South Africa as a whole led him to

---

45. Keith Clements, *A Patriotism for Today: Love of Country in Dialogue with the Witness of Dietrich Bonhoeffer* (London: Collins, 1986), 53.

a dramatic rejection of Apartheid, his ejection from his own church of which he was an esteemed leader, and to his participation in the liberation struggle associated with the ANC. Naudé was South Africa's Bonhoeffer.[46]

No one has symbolized this genuine love for his nation and the wider world than Mandela who, for multitudes, has become the icon of the struggle for justice for all and the reconciliation of former enemies. His aim was not to liberate South Africa at the expense of some, but to set it free for all. Likewise, his aim was not to make South Africa strong at the expense of other nations, but as a beacon of hope for all.

For a nation to aspire to greatness, it always requires such courageous prophets who are prepared to be unpopular in reminding us of the demands of justice, equity, and freedom—prophets who speak the truth out of love for the nation and its peoples to whom they are committed. They will not be surprised if they experience rejection. But they are the best patriots because they know better than most what a country really needs, what true peace and reconciliation require, and above all else, they know about the righteousness that exalts a nation. True patriots do not say "my country right or wrong"; they exercise critical judgment as

46. John W. de Gruchy, "Patriotism: True and False—Reflections on Bonhoeffer, Oom Bey and the Flag," in *Many Cultures, One Nation: Festschrift for Beyers Naudé*, ed. Charles Villa-Vicencio and Carl Niehaus (Cape Town: Human & Rousseau, 1995), 55–68.

responsible citizens. Only such citizens truly stand firm in times of crisis such as ours.

On Christmas Eve 1942, shortly before his arrest the following year, Bonhoeffer presented a gift to his co-conspirators, it was a lengthy document titled "After Ten Years." In it he reflected back over the previous decade in which Hitler had come to power and led Germany into war. He begins with two questions. The first is this: "Have there ever been people in history who in their time, like us, had so little ground under their feet, people to whom every possible alternative open to them at the time appeared equally unbearable, senseless, and contrary to life?" Bonhoeffer's second question follows: "Who stands firm?" His answer to this second question is startling:

> only the one who whose ultimate standard is not his reason, his principles, conscience, freedom or virtue; only the one who is prepared to sacrifice all of these when, in faith and in relationship to God alone, he is called to obedient and responsible action.[47]

So, then, Bonhoeffer asks, "Where are these responsible ones?" Those who stand firm in desperate times? They are those, he says, who exercise their freedom by acting responsibly not by trying to remain "pure"; those who are willing to take both physical and moral risks for the greater good. This does not mean that

47. Bonhoeffer, *Letters and Papers from Prison*, 40.

reason, principle, conscience, freedom, or virtue are not necessary or important. They certainly were for Bonhoeffer as they are for all Christians and people of moral virtue. But Bonhoeffer was aware of how they had been abused in Germany, providing an excuse for doing nothing, or even a rationale for doing something evil. By contrast, for Bonhoeffer, the person who stands firm, the prophet and true patriot, has learned "to see the great events of world history from below, from the perspective of the outcasts, the suspects, the maltreated, the powerless, the oppressed and reviled, in short from the perspective of the suffering."[48]

A constant thread that runs through these pages is that right-wing nationalism is inherently violent whether in its attempt to seize power by force or through democratic means. Such nationalism is always polarizing people, even creating enemies when none actually exist. It is energized by the will-to-power and believes that *Realpolitik* is the only politics. Such nationalism will sometimes more readily pursue the policies of war than peaceful diplomacy. And it can only be overcome by energetic resistance, preferably by peaceful protest as Mahatma Gandhi, Albert Luthuli, and Martin Luther King Jr. pursued; or, in exceptional circumstances when all other options appear closed, by an armed struggle, the choice made by Nelson Mandela, or the terrible choice made by Bonhoeffer and his compatriots.

48. Ibid., 52.

Democracies came into being as an alternative way of doing politics. However flawed and fragile, the democratic path is not violent confrontation and revolution but the ballot-box, and while public protest is often an essential element in bringing about change in government, its touchstone is elections that are free and fair. Power must change hands nonviolently. That is why democracy always seeks to limit exceptional circumstances that require drastic action, promoting diplomacy, dialogue, and strategic compromises as an alternative to violence and war. It may be a more complex process, more demanding in many respects, but resorting to violence and war, apart from its ghastly consequences, seldom resolves the problems that evoke them without creating more problems. In a democracy that is seeking to be just there should never be the need to resort to extreme measures such as Bonhoeffer and Mandela were finally forced to take. That is why there is always the need for civic vigilance, and prophets who speak truth to power before it is too late.

As Europe embarked on a frenzied program of rearmament in the 1930s, Bonhoeffer became actively involved in ecumenical attempts to promote peace through the churches. For him, the ecumenical movement had a divine mandate to work against rearmament and use its international character to reduce the danger of war. Most famously, he spoke to these concerns at the Ecumenical Council of Christian Churches

Conference, held at Fanø, Denmark, in 1934. In his address, Bonhoeffer asked with considerable passion:

> How does peace come about? Through a system of political treaties? Through the investment of international capital in different countries? Through the big banks, through money? Or through universal peaceful rearmament in order to guarantee peace? Through none of these, for the single reason that in all of them peace is confused with safety. There is no way to peace along the way of safety. For peace must be dared. It can never be made safe.[49]

Bonhoeffer's peace witness, and his challenge to the ecumenical church to be bolder in doing so, not least because of its international character reaching across national borders, remains a challenge to the churches in these critical times resembling the 1930s.

"Blessed are the peacemakers," Jesus said. He did not say "peace lovers," but those who actively pursue peace. Both Mandela and Bonhoeffer were essentially such peacemakers. That is why they struggled so hard to avoid resorting to violence. For them peace had to be dared; it was a risky path, a costly path, because it meant standing firm for justice and opposing oppression, it meant rejecting racism and pursuing reconciliation, it meant respecting others even if they were dif-

---

49. Bonhoeffer, "The Church and the Peoples of the World," address to the Ecumenical Council of Christian Churches Conference, Fanø, Denmark, 1934, in *London: 1933-1935*, Dietrich Bonhoeffer Works, vol. 13 (Minneapolis: Fortress Press, 2007), 308–9.

ferent. And, in the end, it meant discovering a source of strength beyond themselves. For only when we do that can we stand firm as we live in these times before the end.

In concluding his celebrated book *After Virtue,* the philosopher Alasdair MacIntyre reminds the reader about the "Dark Ages" that descended on Europe after the fall of Rome. MacIntyre was writing twenty years before the dawning of the new millennium, but with foreboding, not hopeful expectation. Already, he sensed the coming of a new Dark Age, which many fear is now upon us. But he was also looking for clues in that ancient past that could help us find our way in times such as these, when "barbarism and darkness" seem to be gaining the upper hand. His concluding message is one we should heed. "What matters at this stage," he wrote, "is the construction of local forms of community within which civility and moral life can be sustained."[50] We are waiting, he continued, for the likes of a new though perhaps different St. Benedict, that contemplative-activist we have previously encountered in these pages, who can help build communities of hope in which a new generation of committed citizens can be nurtured for these despairing times.

---

50. Alasdair MacIntyre, *After Virtue* (Notre Dame: Notre Dame University Press, 1981), 245.

Postscript: Awaiting the Second Advent

Without prophecy, the language of contemplation runs the risk of detachment from the history in which God is acting and in which we encounter God. Without the mystical dimension, the language of prophecy can narrow its vision and weaken its perception of that which makes all things new.

—Gustavo Gutiérrez[1]

I believe that in every moment of distress God will give us as much strength to resist as we need. . . . I believe that even our mistakes and shortcomings are not in vain and that it is not more difficult for God to deal with them than with our supposedly good deeds. I believe

1. Gustavo Gutiérrez, *The Truth Shall Make You Free: Confrontations* (Maryknoll, NY: Orbis, 1990), 17.

that God is no timeless fate but waits for and responds
to sincere prayer and responsible actions.

—Bonhoeffer[2]

Living in these penultimate times, we await the Second
Advent. Some will interpret that literally, others
metaphorically. What I have suggested throughout
these pages is that it means always living with the end
in mind; whether that be the end of the world as we
know it, the end of our individual lives, or the meaning
and goal of life. Put in other words, it is living in expectation and hope. Christians cannot prove that their
hope will be fulfilled, they can only point to the witness of Scripture and to the countless men and women
who, through the centuries, have lived in hope and
therefore contributed to the well-being of others in
the struggle for justice and peace. Not everyone, by
any means, who has lived and acted in hope has been
a Christian, but their combined example inspires us
today in living and acting with courage and expectation. This is how we await the Second Advent, believing
as Christians, that in the end all things will find their
fulfillment in God.

The prophets to whom I have referred in these pages
were part of that illustrious company. They often
despaired of their fellow human beings who refused
to heed the warnings of the consequences that flow

2. Dietrich Bonhoeffer, *Letters and Papers from Prison*, Dietrich Bonhoeffer
Works, vol. 8 (Minneapolis: Fortress Press, 2010), 46.

from injustice, greed, pride, and violence. There were times when they doubted God and were reduced to silence as they witnessed the disasters and tragedies that ravished the earth and the lives of innocent children, women, and men. Often they were scorned, persecuted, and declared unpatriotic. But somehow they managed to hang on, and often out of the depths they were able to speak a word that brought down the mighty and gave hope to the wretched of the earth. They did not predict the end of the world, but they did, like John the Baptist, point toward the coming of God's reign. They lived and spoke courageously in penultimate times because they were already grasped by the ultimate mystery, God grace, wisdom, and redemptive power.

We therefore fail to grasp the profound relevance of these prophets of ancient and contemporary times who speak to us in these "*kairos* moments" of apocalyptic fear and distress, if we fail to recognize the deep spiritual wells from which they drew and continue to draw their insight and energy. All great prophets have been contemplative activists who, like Dag Hammarskjöld, believed that the "mystical experience" is always "here and now" in that "stillness which is born of silence" where. "the mystery" we name God, "is a constant reality" to those "free from self-concern." For "in our era, the road to holiness passes through the world of action."[3]

3. Dag Hammarskjöld, *Markings* (London: Faber and Faber, 1964), 108.

Contemplative activists know what it means to live in the silence, but their spirituality was deeply rooted in Christian community. For them, being part of a community, whether seen or unseen, in which the life, death and resurrection of Christ is taking form, was fundamental to their lives and witness. This, for Bonhoeffer, was the essence of the church.[4] So it must be in our time, for if the church is to respond faithfully to the challenges of today it has to nourish communities within its life that are able to respond in prayer and action to the challenges facing us;[5] communities of Christians who participate with people of other faiths, or secular humanists, in helping to make this world more compassionate and just, and who nurture the "next generation" in doing so. The Taizé Community in France, the San Engidio Community in Rome, and the global Community of the Cross of Nails centered at Coventry Cathedral in England are among the best known of a growing number of such communities.

In this penultimate time, then, there is much to do as we engage in hopeful action in the struggle for justice and peace as people of faith. With this in mind I return to the words of Bonhoeffer with which I began the Prologue:

4. Bonhoeffer, *Ethics*, Dietrich Bonhoeffer Works, vol. 6, ed. Clifford J. Green (Minneapolis: Fortress Press, 2005), 102.

5. See Bonhoeffer, *Life Together,* Dietrich Bonhoeffer Works, vol. 5 (Minneapolis: Fortress Press, 1996) 128, 133; Bonhoeffer, *Letters and Papers from Prison*, 503.

> What happens here is something penultimate. To give the hungry bread is not yet to proclaim to them the grace of God. . . . But this penultimate thing is related to the ultimate. It is a *pen*-ultimate, before the last. The entry of grace is the ultimate.[6]

Whatever we may do in anticipation of the Second Advent, and there is much to be done, "in the end" we can do no other than trust the God who has become known to us in the death and resurrection of Jesus Christ and in whom all things find fulfillment. This is what it means to be "justified by faith."[7] It is undoubtedly beyond our power to bring in God's kingdom of justice and peace; it is not beyond the power of the Spirit given to us to live and act in anticipation of its coming. Prophets are called to speak the penultimate word and goad us into action in order to prepare the way, but God will always have the last word. To live by faith is to live in expectation that this last word will be the word of grace, for in the end we will be "saved by grace."[8]

6. Bonhoeffer, *Ethics*, 163.
7. Rom 5:1. See Bonhoeffer, *Ethics*, 159–60.
8. Eph 2:5.

Select Bibliography

All quotations from the Bible are from the New Revised Standard Version.

Bonhoeffer, Dietrich. *Ethics*. Dietrich Bonhoeffer Works, vol. 6. Edited by Clifford J. Green. Minneapolis: Fortress Press, 2005.

_____. *Letters and Papers from Prison*. Dietrich Bonhoeffer Works, vol. 8. Edited by John W. de Gruchy. Minneapolis: Fortress Press, 2010.

Boesak, Allan. *Kairos, Crisis and Global Apartheid: The Challenge for Prophetic Resistance*. New York: Palgrave MacMillan, 2015.

Brown, Archie. *The Myth of the Strong Leader: Political Leadership in the Modern Age*. London: Vintage, 2015.

Das, Satyajit. *A Banquet of Consequences: The Reality of Our Unusually Uncertain Economic Future*. London: Pearson, 2015.

D'Antonio, Michael. *The Truth about Trump*. New York: St. Martin's, 2016.

De Gruchy, John W. *Christianity and Democracy: A Theology for a Just World Order*. Cambridge: Cambridge University Press, 1995.

_____. *Being Human: Confessions of a Christian Humanist*. London: SCM, 2006.

_____. *Led into Mystery: Faith Seeking Answers in Life and Death*. London: SCM, 2013.

Elshtain, Jean Bethke. *Democracy on Trial*. New York: HarperCollins, 1995.

Fischer, Klaus P. *Nazi Germany: A New History*. New York: Continuum, 1998.

Forsyth, P. T. *The Justification of God: Lectures for War-Time on a Christian Theodicy*. London: Independent Press, 1948.

Hick, John. *Evil and the Love of God*. London: Macmillan Fontana, 1968.

Hobsbawm, E. J. *Nations and Nationalism Since 1780: Programme, Myth, Reality*. Cambridge: Cambridge University Press, 1992.

Koester, Craig R. *Revelation and the End of All Things*. Grand Rapids: Eerdmans, 2002.

LaCugna, Catherine Mowry. *God for Us: The Trinity and Christian Life*. San Francisco: HarperCollins, 1991.

Mishra, Pankaj. *Age of Anger: A History of the Present*. London: Allen Lane, 2017.

Moltmann, Jürgen. *The Trinity and the Kingdom of God*. London: SCM, 1981.

Newell, Waller. *Tyrants: a History of Power, Injustice, &* *Terror.* Cambridge: Cambridge University Press, 2016.

Niebuhr, Reinhold. *The Children of Light and the Children of Darkness.* New York: Scribner's, 1944.

Saul, John Ralston. *The Collapse of Globalism.* London: Atlantic, 2005.

Stern, Fritz. *The Politics of Cultural Despair: A Study in the Rise of Germanic Ideology.* New York: Doubleday, 1965.

Terreblanche, Sampie. *Western Empires, Christianity, and the Inequalities Between the West and the Rest 1500-2010.* Johannesburg: Random House-Penguin, 2014.

Index of Subjects